INSIDE LEBANON

INSIDE LEBANON

Journey to a Shattered Land with Noam and Carol Chomsky

Essays by Noam Chomsky, Mona el-Farra, Irene Gendzier, Laila el-Haddad, Assaf Kfoury, Jennifer Loewenstein, Hanady Salman, Rasha Salti, and Fawwaz Traboulsi

Photographs by Carol Chomsky and press agencies

Edited by

Assaf Kfoury

AAKAR

INSIDE LEBANON:
Journey to a Shattered Land with Noam and Carol Chomsky

Published in agreement with Monthly Review Press, New York
for sale only in the Indian Subcontinent (India, Pakistan,
Bangladesh, Nepal, Maldives, Bhutan & Sri Lanka)

First Published in India, 2007

ISBN 978-81-89833-28-2 (Pb)

Published by
AAKAR BOOKS
28 E Pocket IV, Mayur Vihar Phase I, Delhi-110 091
Phone : 011-2279 5505 Telefax : 011-2279 5641
aakarbooks@gmail.com; www.aakarbooks.com

Printed at
Mudrak, 30 A Patparganj, Delhi-110 091

Contents

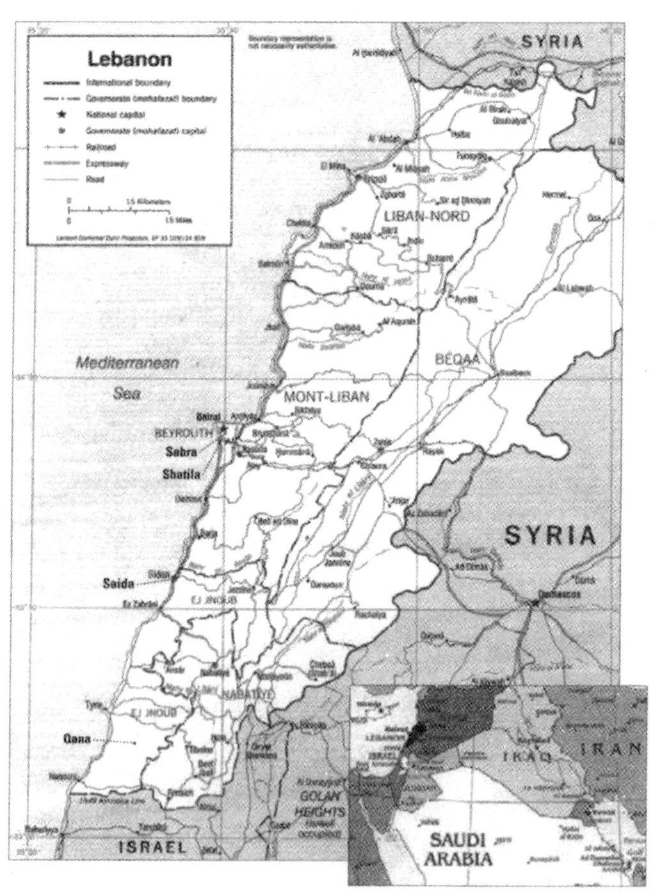
Lebanon
International boundary
Governorate (mohafazat) boundary
National capital
Governorate (mohafazat) capital
Railroad
Expressway
Road
SYRIA
LIBAN-NORD
Tripoli
El Mina
Mediterranean
Sea
BEQAA
MONT-LIBAN
Beirut
BEYROUTH
Sabra
Shatila
Saida
Sidon
EJ JNOUB
NABATIYE
Tyre
Qana
GOLAN
HEIGHTS
ISRAEL
SYRIA
Damascus
IRAQ
IRAN
SAUDI
ARABIA

Preface

Irene Gendzier, Assaf Kfoury, and Fawwaz Traboulsi

We initially planned this book as a written record of Noam and Carol Chomsky's eight-day trip to Lebanon in May 2006. We had planned to collect the texts of Noam's lectures and of an interview that he gave in Beirut, to include a selection of Carol's photos, and to incorporate complementary essays by those of us—Irene Gendzier, Assaf Kfoury, and Fawwaz Traboulsi—who accompanied them throughout their trip.

We started to collect and write the different parts of the book in May and June 2006. For a few weeks, Lebanon seemed a relatively quiet corner of the Middle East, notwithstanding its sharp internal divisions. But there was no escape from the reality of a Lebanon that was but just one place in a patchwork of regional conflicts, raging or suppressed. The carnage in Iraq was relentless; the war on the Palestinians was more intense than ever; the standoff between the West and Iran cast a dark shadow on the entire region. A new Israeli assault on Gaza came on June 28, and a thirty-four-day all-out war on Lebanon began on July 12.

In late July and August 2006, the shock-and-awe campaign against Lebanon was front-page news, day in and day out, though largely covered in isolation as if unrelated to the conflicts nearby. The Western media consensus seemed to ignore the wider Middle East conflict and its impact on Lebanon. Expressions of outrage were narrowly focused on Hezbollah's "reckless provocation," and Israel's brutal response was repeatedly justified, even when qualified as "disproportionate."

There was very little about Lebanon's relation to Palestine, Iraq, the region, and the rest of the world. Only scant objection was offered to what was in the final analysis a campaign supplied and authorized by the U.S. government, though executed by its local Israeli enforcers, to bring Lebanon to heel.

As a result, our conception of *Inside Lebanon* changed, as we sought to give some context to the events that transpired in Lebanon. Noam Chomsky's lectures, interview, and essay illuminate the global dimensions and roots of the conflicts in the Middle East. Fawwaz Traboulsi's closing essay reflects upon the shifting conceptions—by the West—of the Middle East, which are meant to obfuscate global relationships of oppression. Collectively, these writings provide the background for understanding the region-wide conflict, of which Lebanon is only one piece. Assaf Kfoury documents Noam and Carol Chomsky's travels in Lebanon, including a meeting with the secretary-general of Hezbollah, Sayyid Hassan Nasrallah. Irene Gendzier's essay provides an account of their visit to a refugee camp, which was the site of a massacre in 1982, and Khiam prison. Her narrative is filled with reflections regarding the history of these places and Lebanon in general. Carol Chomsky's photographs reveal a Lebanon just months before the Israeli air force reduced these places to rubble—as seen in the photos accompanying the war diaries. We included personal accounts from those who directly experienced the bombing and the destruction during the summer of 2006. Excerpts from the war diaries of Hanady Salman, Rasha Salti, Mona el-Farra, and Laila el-Haddad were collected and assembled. Hanady Salman and Rasha Salti remained in Beirut throughout the thirty-four-day war of July-August 2006. Mona el-Farra and Laila el-Haddad relate many of the daily ordeals suffered by Palestinians through the simultaneous wars in Lebanon and Gaza during the summer of 2006. Jennifer Loewenstein's essay is a reminder that, while people in southern Lebanon are now once more digging out from under the rubble of their ruined homes, the campaign of strangulation and dispossession against the Palestinians continues unabated.

~

We would like to recognize those who helped in the production of this book. Mirna Mneimneh transcribed Noam Chomsky's interview with Marcel Ghanem of LBC television, and Bernhard Geyer of the New York Guggenheim Foundation translated it. Jennifer Loewenstein helped edit the transcription of the interview, as well as selected and edited excerpts from Hanady Salman's diary. Assaf Kfoury selected and edited the excerpts from Mona el-Farra's and Laila el-Haddad's diaries, and translated Fawwaz Traboulsi's essay from the Arabic original. Brett Clark and the folks at Monthly Review Press ably supervised the organization of the texts included in *Inside Lebanon*. The three of us selected photographs from Carol Chomsky's collection (from May 2006) and Hanady Salman's collection (from July–August 2006), and produced the timeline.

February 2007

Beit Eddine. The Chomskys and *al Wafd al Murafiq* ("the accompanying delegation"); from left to right: Carol Chomsky, Irene Gendzier, Noam Chomsky, Fawwaz Traboulsi, and Assaf Kfoury. (photo by Carol Chomsky)

1

Noam and Carol Chomsky in Beirut

Assaf Kfoury

A preliminary version of this essay was posted on the ZNet website on July 12, 2006, under the title "Noam Chomsky in Beirut."

Noam and Carol Chomsky arrived in Beirut on May 8, 2006, for an eight-day visit, their first ever to Lebanon. Many of Noam's Lebanese friends had wanted this visit to happen for a long time. For nearly four decades, the Palestinians and the people of the wider Middle East have all been central among Noam's many concerns. He has written about them and defended them, publicly and tirelessly, and will continue "as long as I'm ambulatory."[1] Beirut gave Noam Chomsky a hero's welcome.

An invitation from the American University in Beirut (AUB) provided the occasion. Noam gave two lectures at the AUB on two consecutive days, May 9 and 10. The rest of the eight-day stay was devoted to meeting people and visiting places.[2] Writer, political activist, and longtime friend Fawwaz Traboulsi organized, with help from me, the non-AUB part of the visit.

Noam's visit came at a time of heightened tension in Lebanon and renewed violence in the Palestinian territories and Iraq. The Western media's recollection of Lebanese events from preceding months was perhaps the assassination of former Lebanese prime minister Rafiq Hariri on February 14, 2005, followed by several massive demonstrations in Beirut during the spring of 2005, which were a major factor in forcing the withdrawal of Syrian troops at the end of April 2005, twenty-nine years after they first entered Lebanon at the beginning of the civil war. Hariri's assassination was still under investigation by a UN-appointed commission. Hariri was a prominent opponent of a three-year extension of Emile Lahoud's presidential mandate, from November 2004 to November 2007, resulting from a constitutional amendment that had been engineered by the Syrian government both by intimidation and through its own allies in the Lebanese parliament. In protest, Hariri resigned from the cabinet premiership in October 2004 and joined an increasingly militant anti-Syrian opposition, whose most vocal leader was Walid Jumblat.

The huge demonstrations in the spring of 2005 were fueled not only by a long-simmering resentment of heavy-handed Syrian domination, but also by a stagnant economy reflected by a staggering national debt estimated at around $40 billion, amounting to more than 180 percent of the country's GDP, one of the highest ratios anywhere in the world. If anything, these demonstrations showed a popular demand for change, mobilizing more than a half-million people (on March 8, 2005) and three quarters of a million (on March 14, 2005) in a country with a population under four million. But the political elites were divided, chiefly according to what they perceived as the main external threat to Lebanon. The organizers of the March 8 demonstration, led by Hezbollah, considered the chief danger to come from Israeli incursions and regional designs, backed by a totally unfettered U.S. policy to reshape the Middle East political map under the Bush administration. In contrast, the organizers of the March 14 demonstration, including Walid Jumblat and others among Rafiq Hariri's allies, argued that the Lebanese first have to free themselves from the danger in their midst—namely, Syria's continued meddling through its local allies and the security agencies it created or molded during its twenty-nine-year military presence—before they could tackle their other problems, including Israeli threats.

In the months following spring 2005, political alliances quickly shifted. The most prominent among these was the switch of the Free Patriotic Movement, led by former army chief Michel Aoun, from the "March 14" coalition to the "March 8" coalition. In spite of the shifting alliances, the two coalitions remained the two main contending poles, at least within the political establishment. The extra-parliamentary left, represented by the Communist Party and several other allied groups, at first seemed eclipsed by the overwhelming events of spring 2005. In subsequent months, however, the Communist Party and its allies took a more assertive role and tended to side with Hezbollah and the March 8 coalition, without being part of it, while a few dissidents split and became part of the March 14 coalition.

Noam and Carol's visit to Lebanon followed on the heels of these political developments. In the spring of 2006, Fawwaz Traboulsi prepared a program of activities for them beyond the AUB lectures. Noam and Carol spent an entire morning in the Sabra-Shatila refugee camp on the outskirts of Beirut, traveled to the Lebanese-Israeli border region, visited the former Israeli prison and torture compound in the town of Khiam in southern Lebanon, and had lengthy meetings with Hezbollah leaders (from the March 8 coalition), with parliamentarian Walid Jumblat and lawyer Chibli Mallat (from the March 14 coalition), and with leaders of the Communist Party. In a seminar at the Lebanese American University on "Palestine 1948," hosted by Fawwaz Traboulsi, Noam engaged the students in a discussion of Zionism and the history of the Israeli-Palestinian conflict. Noam also gave dozens of interviews, for newspapers and TV stations, both Lebanese and non-Lebanese.

In addition to the two AUB lectures to eager, overflowing crowds, Noam gave a third talk to a packed audience at Masrah al Madina, a large movie theatre in Beirut. This latter event was organized by *al Liqaa* (the "Encounter"), a progressive cultural association, introduced by its president, Ghassan Issa, and chaired by Fawwaz Traboulsi. Noam's talk, entitled "Imminent Crises: Threats and Opportunities," dealt with current dangers resulting from the interventionist zeal of the United States in the Middle East.

Just as significant as the planned activities were the countless chance encounters with people—in the street, in the hotel lobby, on the way to a lecture or after, at a meeting enlarged to include other eager participants—who would invariably give Noam a warm welcome: a Palestinian pharmacist in his makeshift drugstore in Sabra-Shatila, a Palestinian labor leader, a former Lebanese cabinet minister, a man rushing to get an inscription on a freshly-bought copy of Noam's *Failed States*, and many others.

Memorable Moments

Fawwaz Traboulsi, Irene Gendzier, and I accompanied Noam and Carol Chomsky throughout their stay May 8–16, along with journalists and filmmakers who documented various parts of the trip. The following is a small selection of the memorable moments from our collective travel notes:

May 11, Sabra-Shatila camp. At the vocational center run by the Palestinian aid and relief association Najda, there are two young university graduates—a Briton and a Palestinian—who teach teenagers how to use computers and connect to the Internet. The Briton volunteer will soon return to the United Kingdom, having completed one year working in the camp. The Palestinian volunteer has a degree in computer science from one of the Lebanese universities, but he has not yet found any employment. A conversation ensues between Noam and the young Palestinian. Noam asks who paid for his university education (UNRWA, a UN agency, paid); whether he looked for a job outside the camp (he did, but in vain); and why no one hired him (employers seemed to prefer Lebanese graduates). "And what, in the long run, if you don't find a job?," Noam asks. "I hope to leave Lebanon," he says. Then with a faint smile, he adds, "Maybe I will become like Edward Said."

In the camp, there is a plot of land, perhaps less than a half acre, surrounded by a wall with a large iron gate, where the victims of the 1982 massacre are buried.[3] The land is mostly flat and covered by grass, with a few mounds here and there. Through the gate's vertical bars, we can see these mass graves. On the outside wall there are large, slightly fading, poster photos of those found dead after the 1982 rampage when Phalangist militiamen, sent by the Israeli army, surrounded the camp. The gatekeeper is an old Palestinian, with half of his teeth missing, sitting under the shade of the tree near the gate, selling flowers. We ask him to open the gate and let us enter the grounds. The old man says that if the visitors are American he will not let them enter. "Yes, the visitors are American, but they are good Americans," I explain. Then, pointing to Noam a few steps away, I say that he, in particular, is the most indefatigable defender of Palestinian rights in America. The old man stares at me with a skeptical look for a few seconds, as if to gauge the truth of what I just said, then gets up and opens the gate.

May 11, Hezbollah headquarters, Beirut. We meet with Sayyid Hassan Nasrallah, the head of Hezbollah, in a heavily fortified compound. Hezbollah has widespread popular support, with representation in the Lebanese parliament and the council of ministers, largely owing to its role in the successful resistance to the Israeli occupation of southern Lebanon in the 1990s. Nevertheless, American government officials—from Condoleezza Rice, David Welch, Elliott Abrams, Jeffrey Feltman, and on down—routinely visit other Lebanese politicians and dignitaries, never Nasrallah, and they portray Hezbollah as a band of terrorists. The value of this meeting with Noam lies as much in what Nasrallah has to say as it does in the public recognition by a prominent American, admittedly the most dissident of them, of Hezbollah's role in Lebanon and the Middle East. Nasrallah recognizes the value of trying to break the official American embargo. He has no objection to Noam quoting him on anything he has said, and his last question to Noam is a request for advice on what Hezbollah can do to counter the pernicious propaganda in the United States.

In response, Noam points out the importance of separating policies emanating from Washington from public opinion in the United States, as the latter is often at odds with the former. He also points out that officials in Washington are usually elected by a minority of the population and represent two parties that are virtually indistinguishable on fundamental issues, hence the importance of reaching out to the U.S. public rather than policymakers who are beholden to corporate interests.

Nasrallah covers a wide range of issues in his presentation, including the arms of Hezbollah, which the United States and its allies have demanded be relinquished. Nasrallah presents Hezbollah's arms in the context of a strategy to defend southern Lebanon, which, he argues, concerns all Lebanese and not only Hezbollah. After the meeting, Noam declares to the pack of journalists and television crews waiting outside: "I think Nasrallah has a reasoned and persuasive argument that the arms should be in the hands of Hezbollah as a deterrent to potential aggression, and there are plenty of background reasons for that. . . ." This statement alone is enough to feed the right-wing rumor mill for a long time to come.

May 12, Masrah al Madina, Beirut. After Noam's lecture, there is an unexpected and particularly poignant moment. A young woman in her late twenties, comes up to Noam and just says, "I am Kinda." She has one of Noam's books, *Pirates and Emperors*, wherein he reproduced the letter she wrote at seven years old, after an American air raid destroyed her home in Tripoli, Libya in April 1986. This was a terrorist attack that killed between sixty and one hundred civilians, aptly characterized by American journalist Donald Neff at the time as "a demonstration of the bully [the Reagan administration] on the block picking a fight with the little guy [the Qaddafi regime]." Kinda asks Noam to sign the book; her mother is there too. Noam calls Carol over and they all meet.

Kinda's letter read:

> Dear Mr. Reagan
> Why did you kill my only sister Rafa and my friend Racha, she is only nine, and my baby doll Strawberry. Is it true you want to kill us all because my father is

Palestinian and you want to kill Kadafi because he wants to help us go back to my father's home and land.
My name is Kinda

ABC correspondent Charles Glass, who reported the Libya bombing and aftermath from the scene in April 1986, dug out Kinda's letter from the rubble of her home. He visited and remained in touch with her American-educated family after they moved to Lebanon.[4]

May 13, Khiam, South Lebanon. To reach Khiam, we drive along a narrow road on the Israeli-Lebanese border that is occasionally marked by a barbed-wire fence. On a bright spring day, we pass the Israeli town of Metulla, where we see some of the inhabitants tending to their daily chores, with houses clustering the hill upon which sits a watchtower with an Israeli flag. This is the uppermost part of Galilee with deep mountain ravines, streams, and lush green fields in May. The view from Khiam across the valley, toward the Shebaa Farms[5] and Mount Hermon at a distance, is breathtaking.

Sheikh Nabil Qauq, head of Hezbollah in southern Lebanon, is waiting for us at the entrance to the former Israeli prison and torture camp in Khiam, surrounded by a bevy of TV crews and journalists. Qauq gives us an effusive reception as soon as we alight from our cars, with Noam getting a warm embrace and kisses on both cheeks. There are two disabled and rusting military trucks with Hebrew markings parked in the middle of the prison yard, left behind by the Israeli army after its withdrawal in May 2000. Photographers and TV cameramen capture the whole scene, but they are not the only ones watching. There is a constant drone overhead—it is an unmanned aircraft barely visible in the bright hazy sky. We are told that the Israeli military regularly flies over the border region to film the movements of suspected Lebanese and Palestinian militants. (The next day, all of Beirut's major newspapers feature front-page photographs of Noam and Qauq inspecting an old Khiam prison cell. Two or three days later, hysterical bloggers proclaim: "Noam Chomsky applauds jihad"; "Chomsky should not be allowed back into the US"; and the usual right-wing Chomsky-bashing diatribes.)

May 13, Nabatiyeh, South Lebanon. Noam is scheduled to appear in an "open discussion" at the Cultural Council for South Lebanon. We are in friendly territory, in more than one sense: the Cultural Council is a bastion of activists of the secular left. The Cultural Council's longtime secretary, Habib Sadek, is a well-known activist for progressive causes in Lebanon.

Habib Sadek starts his introduction: "Today is an historic occasion...as we welcome the most distinguished contemporary linguist, one of the most brilliant progressive thinkers, a symbol of the internationalist left. . . ." The audience's jubilant applause causes a long interruption. "Noam Chomsky keeps reminding us that the true intellectual is the one who defends the rights of the oppressed..." more thundering applause, "...and the one who stands up to the juggernaut of the oppressive state. . . ." Again, interruption and applause.

We have to listen carefully to catch all of Habib Sadek's words and those of subsequent speakers, through the cacophony of constantly moving chairs, repeated applause, and an unruly sound system. The meeting turns into a rather rowdy and enthusiastic gathering, cut short after an hour, at the end of an exhausting day. Approximately one hundred of Nabatiyeh's townspeople, old in suits and young in jeans and colorful shirts, are crowding a small hall to ask questions and hear the honored guest. Outside in the garden, there are at least as many people, some peering through the open windows and doors, others standing back and listening to the exchange inside the hall from the loudspeakers. At the end Habib Sadek, a gaunt and elegantly dressed man in his seventies, bemoans to me about the brevity of the event and the missed opportunity for a longer discussion with Noam.

May 14, Beirut. A delegation of the Lebanese Communist Party (CP) comes to meet Noam at the hotel. It comprises Maurice Nahra, a longtime labor leader and member of the CP leadership, and a younger CP member along to do the two-way translation between Arabic and English. In his day job, our assigned translator is an employee in one of the government ministries. Press photographers show up unexpectedly. They repeatedly take photos of the meeting, every time forcing our assigned translator to leave the meeting and step away from the cameras—in order not to lose his job. He explains that appearing in a newspaper photo as part of a CP delegation meeting Noam Chomsky would reveal his political identity and displease his superiors at the ministry. Every time he leaves the meeting, Fawwaz and I gladly step in to do an impromptu translation.

On May 9 we had informed Noam of a change in the plans for May 10, because the CP, labor unions, and several allied parties had called for a mass demonstration to protest some governmental draft laws, including a new employment contract detrimental to workers. The demonstration was scheduled for May 10 and was likely to paralyze traffic in the city center. We thus proposed a plan that would avoid going through downtown Beirut. Noam asked if we could simply join the demonstration, but we dissuaded him, as a scuffle was likely to break out between the police and the demonstrators.

Noam is now eager to catch up with the news of the demonstration on May 10 and its aftereffects. His questions to Maurice Nahra include: What parties other than the CP and the labor unions were at the demonstration? How large was it? Will it force the government to change some of its draft laws? And if not, what are possible follow-up actions?

Many other invitations and requests for meetings with Noam are made, but not all of these can be accommodated. Some are declined regretfully, such as the request from Ayatollah Muhammad Hussein Fadlallah in recognition of Noam's denunciation of a murderous terrorist attack in March of 1985, now nearly forgotten in the West: a car-bomb operation was organized by the CIA in a populous section of West Beirut with the intent to assassinate Fadlallah. Although Fadlallah escaped serious injury, the bomb killed eighty civilians and wounded over two hundred.[6]

Other invitations are ignored, such as one from a high government official in Syria asking Noam to visit Damascus. This is not the time to even acknowledge such an invitation; on this very day, the Syrian government has arrested the writer and democracy activist Michel Kilo.[7]

May 15, Moukhtara. After a long drive through the Shouf mountains, with two intermediary stops in the towns of Deir al-Qamar and Beit Eddine to visit ancient houses and monuments from the time of the Ottoman empire and before, we reach Moukhtara, nearly 3,000 feet above sea level. Moukhtara is the home village of the Jumblat family, whose generations-old residence is a majestic mansion—with high ceilings and arches, all in grey stone, and stained glass windows typical of this region of the world—perched on a promontory overlooking a lush verdant valley.

Walid Jumblat is waiting for us at the entrance court, along with Chibli Mallat, a prominent Beirut lawyer and now a candidate for the Lebanese presidency. Both Jumblat and Mallat are part of the pro-government "March 14" coalition, and Jumblat is perhaps its most forceful politician. Jumblat invites us for a lavish lunch, followed by a long conversation with him and Mallat. Jumblat does not mince words when talking about the Syrian regime. He recounts many assassinations carried out on orders from the Syrian government since the 1970s, including that of his father Kamal Jumblat in 1977. We try to elicit from both Jumblat and Mallat some constructive suggestions for the future of Lebanon, and the region, but these seem elusive given the many difficulties. Mallat is interested in Noam's recommendations to the Lebanese parties on how to resolve their current political crisis. Noam sensibly points out it is not for him to instruct Lebanese on their problems and, more generally, stresses the destructive effects of inviting outsiders to interfere in internal Lebanese affairs.

~

Noam and Carol's eight-day visit to Lebanon served as the basis for many important connections. For those who welcomed Noam in Beirut, it was significant to hear an American voice of hope and reason, however briefly, in contrast to the unending ominous pronouncements from Washington officials that are in effect promises for more violence and destruction—in Lebanon, the Palestinian territories, Iraq, and the Middle East in general. For Noam, his short visit was important too, giving him firsthand experience with people and places that have been at the center of his concerns for many decades. It was an extraordinary visit at a particularly tense moment in the Middle East.

Nabatiyeh. Noam Chomsky between Habib Sadek and Fawwaz Traboulsi. (photo by Carol Chomsky)

2

Imminent Crises: Threats and Opportunities

Noam Chomsky

On May 12, 2006, Noam Chomsky delivered "Imminent Crises: Threats and Opportunities" as a lecture at Masrah al Madina, a large movie theatre in the Hamra district in Beirut. The event was organized by al Liqaa *("The Encounter"), a Beirut-based progressive cultural and political association.*

Regrettably, there are all too many candidates that qualify as imminent and very serious crises. Several should be high on everyone's agenda of concern, because they pose literal threats to human survival: the increasing likelihood of a terminal nuclear war, and environmental disaster, which may not be too far removed. However, I would like to focus on narrower issues, those that are of greatest concern in the West right now. I will be speaking primarily of the United States, which I know best, and it is the most important case because of its enormous power. But as far as I can ascertain, Europe is not very different.

The area of greatest concern is the Middle East. There is nothing novel about that. I often have to arrange talks years in advance. If I am asked for a title, I suggest "The Current Crisis in the Middle East." It has yet to fail. There's a good reason: the huge energy resources of the region were recognized by Washington sixty years ago as a "stupendous source of strategic power," the "strategically most important area of the world," and "one of the greatest material prizes in world history."[1] Control over this stupendous prize has been a primary goal of U.S. policy ever since, and threats to it have naturally aroused enormous concern.

For years it was pretended that the threat was from the Russians, the routine pretext for violence and subversion all over the world. In the case of the Middle East, we do not have to consider this pretext, since it was officially abandoned. When the Berlin Wall fell, the first Bush administration released a new National Security Strategy, explaining that everything would go as before but within a new rhetorical framework. The massive military system is still necessary, but now because of the "technological sophistication of third world powers"—which at least comes closer to the truth—the primary threat, worldwide, has been indigenous nationalism. The official document explained further that the United States would maintain its intervention forces aimed at the Middle East, where "the threat to our interests" that required intervention "could not be laid at the Kremlin's door," contrary to decades of fabrication.[2] As is normal, all of this passed without comment.

The most serious current problem in the minds of the population, by far, is Iraq. And the easy winner in the competition for the country that is the most feared is Iran, not because Iran really poses a severe threat, but because of a drumbeat of government-media propaganda. That is a familiar pattern. The most recent example is Iraq. The invasion of Iraq was virtually announced in September 2002. As we now know, the U.S.-British invasion was already underway in secret. In that month, Washington initiated a huge propaganda campaign, with lurid warnings by Condoleezza Rice and others that the next message from Saddam Hussein would be a mushroom cloud in New York City. Within a few weeks, the government-media propaganda barrage had driven Americans completely off the international spectrum. Saddam may have been despised almost everywhere, but it was only in the United States that a majority of the population were terrified of what he might do to them, tomorrow. Not surprisingly, support for the war correlated very closely with such fears. That has been achieved before, in amazing ways during the Reagan years, and there is a long and illuminating earlier history. But I will keep to the current monster being crafted by the doctrinal system, after a few words about Iraq.

There is a flood of commentary about Iraq, but very little reporting. Journalists are mostly confined to fortified areas in Baghdad, or embedded within the occupying army. That is not because they are cowards or lazy, but because it is simply too dangerous to be anywhere else. That has not been true in earlier wars. It is an astonishing fact that the United States and Britain have had more trouble running Iraq than the Nazis had in occupied Europe, or the Russians in their East European satellites, where the countries were run by local civilians and security forces, with the iron fist poised if anything went wrong but usually in the background. In contrast, the United States has been unable to establish an obedient client regime in Iraq, under far easier conditions.

Putting aside doctrinal blinders, what should be done in Iraq? Before answering, we should be clear about some basic principles. The major principle is that an invader has no rights, only responsibilities. The first responsibility is to pay reparations. The second responsibility is to follow the will of the victims. There is actually a third responsibility: to bring criminals to trial, but that obligation is so remote from the imperial mentality of Western culture that I will put it aside.

The responsibility to pay reparations to Iraqis goes far beyond the crime of aggression and its terrible aftermath. The United States and Britain have been torturing the population of Iraq for a long time. In recent history, both governments strongly supported Saddam Hussein's terrorist regime through the period of his worst crimes, and long after the end of the war with Iran. Iran finally capitulated, recognizing that it could not fight the United States, which was, by then, openly participating in Saddam's aggression—something that Iranians have surely not forgotten, even if Westerners have. Dismissing history is always a convenient stance for those who hold the clubs, but their victims usually prefer to pay attention to the real world. After the Iran-Iraq war, Washington and London continued to provide military equipment to their friend Saddam, including means to develop weapons of mass destruction and delivery systems. Iraqi nuclear engineers were even being brought to the United States for instruction in developing nuclear weapons in 1989, long after Saddam's worst atrocities and Iran's capitulation. Immediately after the 1991 Gulf War, the United States and United Kingdom returned to their support for Saddam when they effectively authorized him to use heavy military equipment to suppress a Shiite uprising that might well have overthrown the tyrant. The reasons were publicly explained. The *New York Times* reported that there was a "strikingly unanimous view" among the United States and its allies Britain and Saudi Arabia that "whatever the sins of the Iraqi leader, he offered the West and the region a better hope for his country's stability than did those who have suffered his repression"; the term "stability" is a code word for "following orders."[3] *New York Times* chief diplomatic correspondent Thomas Friedman explained that "the best of all worlds" for Washington would be an "iron-fisted military junta" ruling Iraq just the way Saddam did. But lacking that option, Washington had to settle for second-best: Saddam himself. An unthinkable option—then and now—is that Iraqis should rule Iraq independently of the United States.

Then followed the murderous sanctions regime imposed by the United States and Britain, which killed hundreds of thousands of people, devastated

Iraqi civilian society, strengthened the tyrant, and forced the population to rely on him for survival. The sanctions probably saved Saddam from the fate of other vicious tyrants, some quite comparable to him, who were overthrown from within despite strong support from the United States and United Kingdom to the end of their bloody rule: Ceausescu, Suharto, and quite a rogues gallery of others, to which new names are being added regularly. Again, all of this is boring ancient history for those who hold the clubs, but not for their victims, or for people who prefer to understand the world. All of those actions, and much more, call for reparations, on a massive scale, and the responsibility extends to others as well. But the deep moral-intellectual crisis of imperial culture prevents any thought of such topics as these.

The second responsibility is to obey the will of the population. British and U.S. polls provide sufficient evidence about that. The most recent polls find that 87 percent of Iraqis want a "concrete timeline for U.S. withdrawal," up from 76 percent in 2005.[4] If the reports really mean "Iraqis," as they say, that would imply that virtually the entire population of Arab Iraq, where the U.S. and British armies are deployed, wants a firm timetable for withdrawal. I doubt that one would have found comparable figures in occupied Europe under the Nazis, or Eastern Europe under Russian rule.

Bush-Blair and associates declare, however, that there can be no timetable for withdrawal. That stand in part reflects the natural hatred for democracy among the powerful, often accompanied by eloquent calls for democracy. The calls for democracy moved to center stage after the failure to find weapons of mass destruction in Iraq, so a new motive had to be invented for the invasion. The president announced the doctrine to great acclaim in November 2003, at the National Endowment for Democracy in Washington. He proclaimed that the real reason for the invasion was not Saddam's weapons programs, as Washington and London had insistently claimed, but rather Bush's messianic mission to promote democracy in Iraq, the Middle East, and elsewhere. The media and prominent scholars were deeply impressed, relieved to discover that the "liberation of Iraq" is perhaps the "most noble" war in history, as leading liberal commentators announced—a sentiment echoed even by critics, who objected that the "noble goal" may be beyond our means, and those to whom we are offering this wonderful gift may be too backward to accept it. That conclusion was confirmed a few days later by U.S. polls in Baghdad. Asked why the United States invaded Iraq, some agreed with the new doctrine hailed by Western intellectuals: 1 percent agreed that the goal was to promote democracy. Another 5 percent said that the goal was to help Iraqis.[5] Most of the rest took for granted that the goals were the obvious ones that are unmentionable in polite society—the strategic-economic goals we readily attribute to enemies, as when Russia invaded Afghanistan or Saddam invaded Kuwait, but are unmentionable when we turn to ourselves.

But rejection of the popular will in Iraq goes far beyond the natural fear of democracy on the part of the powerful. Simply consider the policies that are likely to be pursued by an independent and more or less democratic Iraq. Iraqis may have no love for Iran, but they would doubtlessly prefer friendly relations with their powerful neighbor. The Shiite majority already has ties to Iran and has been moving to strengthen them. Furthermore, even limited sovereignty in Iraq has encouraged efforts by the harshly repressed Shiite population across the border in Saudi Arabia to gain basic rights and perhaps autonomy. That is where most of Saudi Arabia's oil happens to be.

Such developments might lead to a loose Shiite alliance controlling the world's major energy resources and independent of Washington, the ultimate nightmare in Washington—except that it might get worse: the alliance might strengthen its economic and possibly even military ties with China. The United States can intimidate Europe: when Washington shakes its fist, leading European business enterprises pull out of Iran. But China has a three-thousand-year history of contempt for the barbarians: they refuse to be intimidated.

That is the basic reason for Washington's strategic concerns with regard to China: not that it is a military threat, but that it poses the threat of independence. If that threat is unacceptable for small countries like Cuba or Vietnam, it is certainly so for the heartland of the most dynamic economic region in the world, the country that has just surpassed Japan in possession of the world's major financial reserves, and is the world's fastest growing major economy. China's economy is already about two-thirds the size of that of the United States, by the correct measures, and if current growth rates persist, it is likely to close that gap in about a decade—in absolute terms, not per capita of course.

China is also the center of the Asian Energy Security Grid and the Shanghai Cooperation Organization, which includes the Central Asian countries, and just a few weeks ago was joined by India, Iran, and Pakistan as observers, soon probably members. India is undertaking significant joint energy projects with China, and it might join the Energy Security Grid. Iran may as well, if it comes to the conclusion that Europe is so intimidated by the United States that it cannot act independently. If Iran turns to the East, it will find willing partners. A major conference on energy last September in Tehran brought together government officials and scholars from Iran, China, Pakistan, India, Russia, Egypt, Indonesia, Georgia, Venezuela, and Germany, planning an extensive pipeline system for the entire region and also more intensive development of energy resources. Bush's recent trip to India, and his authorization of India's nuclear weapons program, is part of the jockeying over how these major global forces will crystallize. A sovereign and partially democratic Iraq could be another contribution to developments that seriously threaten U.S. global hegemony, so it is not at all surprising that Washington has sought in every way to prevent such an outcome, joined by "the spear carrier for the *pax Americana*," as Blair's Britain is described by Michael MccGwire in Britain's leading journal of international affairs.[6]

If the United States were compelled to grant some degree of sovereignty to Iraq, and any of these consequences would ensue, Washington planners would be facing the collapse of one of their highest foreign policy objectives since the Second World War, when the United States replaced Britain as the world-dominant power: the need to control "the strategically most important area of the world." What has been central to planning is control, not access, an important distinction. The United States followed the same policies long before it relied on a drop of Middle East oil, and would continue to do so if it relied on solar energy. Such control gives the United States "veto power" over its industrial rivals, as explained in the early postwar period by influential planners, and reiterated recently with regard to Iraq: a successful conquest of Iraq would give the United States "critical leverage" over its industrial rivals, Europe and Asia, as pointed out by Zbigniew Brzezinski, an important figure in the planning community. Vice President Dick Cheney made the same point, describing control over petroleum supplies as "tools of intimidation and blackmail"—when used by others.[7] He went on to urge the dictatorships of Central Asia, Washington's models of democracy, to agree to pipeline construction that ensures that the tools remain in Washington's hands.

The thought is by no means original. At the dawn of the oil age, almost ninety years ago, Britain's first lord of the admiralty, Walter Hume Long, explained that "if we secure the supplies of oil now available in the world we can do what we like."[8] Woodrow Wilson also understood this crucial point. Wilson expelled the British from Venezuela, which by 1928 had become the world's leading oil exporter, with U.S. companies then placed in charge. To achieve this goal, Wilson and his successors supported the vicious and corrupt dictator of Venezuela and ensured that he would bar British concessions. Meanwhile the United States continued to demand—and secure—U.S. oil rights in the Middle East, where the British and French were in the lead.

We might note that these events illustrate the actual meaning of the "Wilsonian idealism" admired by Western intellectual culture, and also provide the real meaning of "free trade" and the "open door." Sometimes that is even officially acknowledged. When the post-Second World War global order was being shaped in Washington, a State Department memorandum on U.S. petroleum policy called for preserving absolute U.S. control of Western hemisphere resources "coupled with insistence upon the Open Door principle of equal opportunity for United States companies in new areas."[9] That is a useful illustration of "really existing free market doctrine": What we have, we keep, closing the door to others; what we do not yet have, we take, under the principle of the Open Door. All of this illustrates the one really significant theory of international relations, the maxim of Thucydides: the strong do as they can, and the weak suffer as they must.

With regard to Iraq today, talk about exit strategies means very little unless these realities are confronted. How Washington planners will deal with these problems is far from clear. And they face similar problems elsewhere. Intelligence projections for the new millennium were that the United States would control Middle East oil as a matter of course, but would itself rely on more stable Atlantic Basin reserves: West African dictatorships' and the Western hemisphere's. But Washington's postwar control of South America, from Venezuela to Argentina, is seriously eroding. The two major instruments of control have been violence and economic strangulation, but each weapon is losing its efficacy. The latest attempt to sponsor a military coup was in 2002, in Venezuela, but the United States had to back down when the government it helped install was quickly overthrown by popular resistance, and there was turmoil in Latin America, where democracy is taken much more seriously than in the West and overthrow of a democratically elected government is no longer accepted quietly. Economic controls are also eroding. South American countries are paying off their debts to the IMF—basically an offshoot of the U.S. Treasury Department. More frightening yet to Washington, these countries are being aided by Venezuela. The president of Argentina announced that the country would "rid itself of the IMF." Rigorous adherence to IMF rules had led to economic disaster, from which the country recovered by radically violating the rules. Brazil too had rid itself of the IMF, and Bolivia probably will as well, again aided by Venezuela. U.S. economic controls are seriously weakening.

Washington's main concern is Venezuela, the leading oil producer in the Western hemisphere. The U.S. Department of Energy estimates that its reserves might be greater than Saudi Arabia's if the price of oil stays high enough for exploitation of its expensive extra-heavy oil to become profitable. Extreme U.S. hostility and subversion has accelerated Venezuela's interest in diversifying exports and investment, and China is more than willing to accept the opportunity, as it is with other resource-rich Latin American exporters. The largest gas reserves in South America are in Bolivia, which is now following much the same path as Venezuela. Both countries pose a problem for Washington in other respects. They have popularly elected governments. Venezuela leads Latin America in support for the elected government, increasing sharply in the past few years under Chávez. He is bitterly hated in the United States because of his independence and enormous popular support. Bolivia just had a democratic election of a kind next to inconceivable in the West. There were serious issues that the population understood very well, and there was active participation of the general population, who elected someone from their own ranks, from the indigenous majority. Democracy is always frightening to power centers, particularly when it goes too far beyond mere form and involves actual substance.

Commentary on what is happening reveals the nature of the fears. London's *Financial Times* warned that President Evo Morales of Bolivia is becoming increasingly "authoritarian" and "undemocratic." This is a serious concern to Western powers, who are dedicated to freedom and democracy everywhere. The proof of his authoritarian stance and departure from democratic principles is that he followed the will of 95 percent of the population and nationalized Bolivia's gas resources, and is also gaining popularity by cutting public salaries and eliminating corruption. Morales's policies have come to resemble the frightening leader of Venezuela. As if the popularity of Chávez's elected government was not proof enough that he is an anti-democratic dictator, he is attempting to extend to Bolivia the same programs he is instituting in Venezuela: helping "Bolivia's drive to stamp out illiteracy and pay[ing] the wages of hundreds of Cuban doctors who have been sent to work there" among the poor, to quote the *Financial Times*'s lament.[10]

The latest Bush administration National Security Strategy, released March 2006, describes China as the greatest long-term threat to U.S. global dominance. The threat is not military, but economic. The document warns that Chinese leaders are not only "expanding trade, but acting as if they can somehow 'lock up' energy supplies around the world or seek to direct markets rather than opening them up."[11] In the U.S.-China meetings in Washington a few weeks ago, President Bush warned President Hu Jintao against trying to "lock up" global supplies. Bush condemned China's reliance on oil from Sudan, Burma, and Iran, accusing China of opposition to free trade and human rights—unlike Washington, which imports only from pure democracies that worship human rights, like Equatorial Guinea, one of the most vicious African dictatorships; Colombia, which has by far the worst human rights record in Latin America; the Central Asian states; and other paragons of virtue. No respectable person would accuse Washington of "locking up" global supplies when it pursues its traditional "open door policy" and outright aggression to ensure that it dominates global energy supplies, firmly holding "the tools of intimidation and blackmail." It is interesting, perhaps, that none of this elicits ridicule in the West, or even notice.

The lead story in the *New York Times* on the Bush-Hu meeting reported that "China's appetite for oil also affects its stance on Iran. . . . The issue [of China's effort to 'lock up' global supplies] is likely to come to a particular head over Iran," where China's state-owned oil giant signed a $70 billion deal to develop Iran's huge Yadavaran oil field.[12] That's a serious matter, compounded by Chinese interference even in Saudi Arabia, a U.S. client state since the British were expelled during the Second World War. This relationship is now threatened by growing economic and military ties between China and the Kingdom of Saudi Arabia, now China's largest trading partner in West Asia and North Africa—perhaps further proof of China's lack of concern for democracy and human rights. When President Hu visited Washington, he was denied a state dinner, in a calculated insult. He cheerfully reciprocated by going directly to Saudi Arabia, a serious slap in the face to Washington that was surely not misunderstood.

This is the barest sketch of the relevant global context over what to do in Iraq. But these critical matters are scarcely mentioned in the ongoing debate about the problem of greatest concern to Americans. They are barred by a rigid doctrine. It is unacceptable to attribute rational strategic-economic thinking to one's own state, which must be guided by benign ideals of freedom, justice, peace, and other wonderful things. That leads back again to a very severe crisis in Western intellectual culture, not of course unique in history, but with dangerous portent.

We can be confident that these matters, though excluded from public discussion, engage the attention of planners. Governments typically regard their populations as a major enemy, and keep them in ignorance of what is happening to them and planned for them. Nevertheless, we can speculate. One reasonable speculation is that Washington planners may be seeking to inspire secessionist movements that the United States can then "defend" against the home country. In Iran, the main oil resources are in the Arab areas adjacent to the Gulf, Iran's Khuzestan—and sure enough, there is now an Ahwazi liberation movement of unknown origin, claiming unspecified rights of autonomy. Nearby, Iraq and the gulf states provide a base for U.S. military intervention.

The U.S. military presence in Latin America is also increasing substantially. In Venezuela, oil resources are concentrated in Zulia province near Colombia, the one reliable U.S. land base in the region, a province that is anti-Chávez and already has an autonomy movement, again of unknown origins. In Bolivia, the gas resources are in richer eastern areas dominated by elites of European descent that bitterly oppose the government elected by the indigenous majority, and have threatened to secede. Nearby Paraguay is another one of the few remaining reliable land bases for the U.S. military. Total military and police assistance now exceeds economic and social aid, a dramatic reversal of the pattern during Cold War years. The U.S. military now has more personnel in Latin America than most key civilian federal agencies combined, again a sharp change from earlier years. The new mission is to combat "radical populism"—the term that is regularly used for independent nationalism that does not obey orders. Military training is being shifted from the State Department to the Pentagon, freeing it from human rights and democracy conditionality under congressional supervision—which was always weak, but had some effects that constrained executive violence.

The United States is a global power, and its policies should not be viewed in isolation, any more than those of the British Empire. Going back half a century, the Eisenhower administration identified three major global problems: Indonesia, North Africa, and the Middle East—all oil producers, all Islamic. In all cases, the concern was independent nationalism. The end of French rule in Algeria resolved the North African problem. In Indonesia, the 1965 Suharto coup removed the threat of independence with a huge massacre, which the CIA compared to the crimes of Hitler, Stalin, and Mao. The "staggering mass slaughter," as the *New York Times* described it, was greeted in the West with unconcealed euphoria and relief.[13] The military coup destroyed the only mass-based political party, a party of the poor, slaughtered huge numbers of landless peasants, and threw the country open to Western exploitation of its rich resources, while the large majority tries to survive in misery. Two years later, the major problem in the Middle East was resolved with Israel's destruction of the Nasser regime, hated by the United States and Britain, which feared that secular nationalist forces might seek to direct the vast energy resources of the region to internal development. A few years earlier, U.S. intelligence had warned of popular feelings that oil is a "national patrimony" exploited by the West by unjust arrangements imposed by force. Israel's service to the United States, its Saudi ally, and the energy corporations confirmed the judgment of U.S. intelligence in 1958 that a "logical corollary" of opposition to Arab nationalism is reliance on Israel as "the only strong pro-Western power in the Middle East," apart from Turkey, which established a close military alliance with Israel in 1958, within the U.S. strategic framework.[14]

The U.S.-Israeli alliance, unique in world affairs, dates from Israel's 1967 military conquests, reinforced in 1970 when Israel barred possible Syrian intervention in Jordan to protect Palestinians who were being slaughtered during Black September. Such intervention by Syria was regarded in Washington as a threat to its ally Jordan and, more important, to the oil-producers that were Washington's clients. U.S. aid to Israel roughly quadrupled. The pattern is fairly consistent since, extending to secondary Israeli services to U.S. power outside the Middle East, particularly in Latin America and southern Africa. The system of domination has worked quite well for the people who matter. Energy corporation profits are breaking all records. High-tech (including military) industry has lucrative ties with Israel, as do the major financial institutions, and Israel serves virtually as an offshore military base and provider of equipment and training. One may argue that other policies would have been more beneficial to the concentrations of domestic power that largely determine policy, but they seem to find these arrangements quite tolerable. If they did not, they could easily move to terminate them. And in fact, when there are conflicts between U.S. and Israeli state power, Israel naturally backs down; exports of military technology to China are a recent example, when the Bush administration went out of its way to humiliate Israel after it was initially reluctant to follow the orders of what Israeli commentator Aluf Benn calls "the boss-man called 'partner.' "

Let us turn next to Iran and its nuclear programs. Until 1979, Washington strongly supported these programs. During those years, of course, a brutal tyrant installed by the U.S.-U.K. military coup that overthrew the Iranian parliamentary government ruled Iran. Today, the standard claim is that Iran has no need for nuclear power, and therefore must be pursuing a secret weapons program. Henry Kissinger explained that "For a major oil producer such as Iran, nuclear energy is a wasteful use of resources." As secretary of state thirty years ago, Kissinger held that "introduction of nuclear power will both provide for the growing needs of Iran's economy and free remaining oil reserves for export or conversion to petrochemicals," and the United States acted to assist the Shah's efforts. Dick Cheney, Donald Rumsfeld, and Paul Wolfowitz, the leading planners of the second Bush administration, worked hard to provide the Shah with a "complete 'nuclear fuel cycle'—reactors powered by and regenerating fissile materials on a self-sustaining basis. That is precisely the ability the current administration is trying to prevent Iran from acquiring today." U.S. universities were arranging to train Iranian nuclear engineers, doubtless with Washington's approval, if not initiative; including my own university, the Massachusetts Institute of Technology, for example, despite overwhelming student opposition. Kissinger was asked about his reversal, and he responded with his usual engaging frankness: "They were an allied country."[15] So therefore they had a genuine need for nuclear energy, pre-1979, but have no such need today.

The Iranian nuclear programs, as far as is known, fall within its rights under Article IV of the Non-Proliferation Treaty (NPT), which grants non-nuclear states the right to produce fuel for nuclear energy. The Bush administration argues, however, that Article IV should be strengthened, and I think that makes sense. When the NPT came into force in 1970, there was a considerable gap between producing fuel for energy and for nuclear weapons. But with contemporary technology, the gap has been narrowed. However, any such revision of Article IV would have to ensure unimpeded access for nonmilitary use, in accord with the initial bargain. A reasonable proposal was put forth by Mohamed ElBaradei, head of the International Atomic Energy Agency: that all production and processing of weapon-usable material be under international control, with "assurance that legitimate would-be users could get their supplies."[16] That should be the first step, he proposed, towards fully implementing the 1993 UN resolution calling for a Fissile Material Cutoff Treaty (called FISSBAN, for short), which bans production of fissile materials by individual states. ElBaradei's proposal was dead in the water. The U.S. political leadership, surely in its current stance, would never agree to this delegation of sovereignty. To date, ElBaradei's proposal has been accepted by only one state, to my knowledge: Iran, last February. That suggests one way to resolve the current crisis—in fact, a far more serious crisis: continued production of fissile materials by individual states is likely to doom humanity to destruction.

Washington also strenuously opposes a verifiable FISSBAN treaty, regarded by specialists as the "most fundamental nuclear arms control proposal," according to Princeton arms controld specialist Frank von Hippel.[17] Despite U.S. opposition, in November 2004 the UN Disarmament Committee voted in favor of a verifiable FISSBAN. The vote was 147 to 1, with 2 abstentions: Israel, which is reflexive, and Britain, which is more interesting. The British ambassador, John Freeman, explained that Britain supported the treaty, but could not vote for this version, he said, because it "divides the international community"—divided it 147 to 1.[18] A later vote in the full General Assembly was 179 to 2, Israel and Britain again abstaining. The United States was joined by Palau.

We gain some insight into the ranking of survival of the species among the priorities of the leadership of the hegemonic power and its spear-carrier.

In 2004, the European Union (EU) and Iran reached an agreement on nuclear issues: Iran agreed to temporarily suspend its legal activities of uranium enrichment, and the EU agreed to provide Iran with "firm commitments on security issues." As everyone understands, the phrase "security issues" refers to the very credible U.S.-Israeli threats and preparations to attack Iran. These threats, a serious violation of the UN Charter, are no small matter for a country that has been tortured for fifty years without a break by the global superpower, which now occupies the countries on Iran's borders, not to speak of the client state that is the regional superpower.

Iran lived up to its side of the bargain, but the EU, under U.S. pressure, rejected its commitments. Iran finally abandoned the bargain as well. The preferred version in the West is that Iran broke the agreement, proving that it is a serious threat to world order.

In May 2003, Iran had offered to discuss the full range of security matters with the United States, which refused, preferring to follow the same course it did with North Korea. On taking office in January 2001, the Bush administration withdrew the "no hostile intent" condition of earlier agreements and proceeded to issue serious threats, while also abandoning promises to provide fuel oil and a nuclear reactor. In response, North Korea returned to developing nuclear weapons, the roots of another current crisis. All predictable, and predicted.

There are ways to mitigate and probably end these crises. The first is to call off the threats that are virtually urging Iran (and North Korea) to develop nuclear weapons. One of Israel's leading military historians, Martin van Creveld, wrote that if Iran is not developing nuclear weapons, then they are "crazy," immediately after Washington demonstrated that it will attack anyone it likes as long as they are known to be defenseless.[19] So the first step towards ending the crisis would be to call off the threats that are likely to lead potential targets to develop a deterrent—where nuclear weapons or terror are the only viable options.

A second step would be to join with other efforts to reintegrate Iran into the global economy. A third step would be to join the rest of the world in accepting a verifiable FISSBAN treaty, and to join Iran in accepting ElBaradei's proposal, or something similar—and I repeat that the issue here extends far beyond Iran, and reaches the level of human survival. A fourth step would be to live up to Article VI of the NPT, which obligates the nuclear states to take "good faith" efforts to eliminate nuclear weapons, a binding legal obligation, as the World Court determined. None of the nuclear states have lived up to that obligation, but the United States is far in the lead in violating it—again, a very serious threat to human survival. Even steps in these directions would mitigate the upcoming crisis with Iran.

Above all, it is important to heed the words of Mohamed ElBaradei: "There is no military solution to this situation. It is inconceivable. The only durable solution is a negotiated solution."[20] And it is within reach. Similar to the Iraq war: a war against Iran appears to be opposed by the military and U.S. intelligence, but might well be undertaken by the civilian planners of the Bush administration: Cheney, Rumsfeld, Rice, and a few others, an unusually dangerous collection.

There is wide agreement among prominent strategic analysts that the threat of nuclear war is severe and increasing, and that the threat can be eliminated by measures that are known and in fact legally obligatory. If such measures are not taken, they warn that "a nuclear exchange is ultimately inevitable," that we may be facing "an appreciable risk of ultimate doom," an "Armageddon of our own making."[21] The threats are well understood, and they are being consciously enhanced. The Iraq invasion is only the most blatant example.

Clinton's military and intelligence planners had called for "dominating the space dimension of military operations to protect U.S. interests and investment," much in the way armies and navies did in earlier years, but now with a sole hegemon, which must develop "space-based strike weapons [enabling] the application of precision force from, to, and through space." Such measures will be needed, they said, because "globalization of the world economy" will lead to a "widening economic divide" along with "deepening economic stagnation, political instability, and cultural alienation," hence unrest and violence among the "have-nots," much of it directed against the United States. The United States must therefore be ready to plan for a "precision strike from space [as a] counter to the worldwide proliferation of WMD" by unruly elements.[22] That is a likely consequence of the recommended military programs, just as a "widening divide" is the anticipated consequence of the specific version of international integration that is misleadingly called "globalization" and "free trade" in the doctrinal system.

A word should be added about these notions. Both are terms of propaganda, not description. The term "globalization" is used for a specific form of international economic integration, designed—not surprisingly—in the interests of the designers: multinational corporations and the few powerful states to which they are closely linked. An opposing form of globalization is being pursued by groups that are far more representative of the world's population, the mass global justice movements, which originated in the South but now have been joined by northern popular organizations and meet annually in the World Social Forum, which has spawned many regional and local social forums, concentrating on their own issues though within the same overarching framework. The global justice movements are an entirely new phenomenon, perhaps the seeds of the kind of international that has been the hope of the workers movements and the left since their modern origins. They are called "antiglobalization" in the reigning doctrinal systems, because they seek a form of globalization oriented towards the interests of people, not concentrated economic power—and unfortunately, they have often adopted this ridiculous terminology.

Official globalization is committed to so-called neoliberalism, also a highly misleading term: the regime is not new, and it is not liberal. Neoliberalism is essentially the policy imposed by force on the colonies since the eighteenth century, while the currently wealthy countries radically violated these rules, with extensive reliance on state intervention in the economy and resort to measures that are now banned in the international economic order. That was true of England and the countries that followed its path of protectionism and state intervention, including Japan, the one country of the South that escaped colonization and the one country that industrialized. These facts are widely recognized by economic historians.

A comparison of the United States and Egypt in the early nineteenth century is one of many enlightening illustrations of the decisive role of sovereignty and massive state intervention in economic development. Having freed itself from British rule, the United States was able to adopt British-style measures of state intervention, and developed. Meanwhile British power was able to bar anything of the sort in Egypt, joining with France to impose Lord Palmerston's doctrine that "No ideas therefore of fairness towards Mehemet [Ali] ought to stand in the way of such great and paramount interests" as barring competition in the eastern Mediterranean.[23] Palmerston expressed his "hate" for the "ignorant barbarian" who dared to undertake economic development. Historical memories resonate when, today, Britain and France, fronting for the United States, demand that Iran suspend all activities related to nuclear and missile programs, including research and development, so that nuclear energy is barred and the country that is probably under the greatest threat of any in the world has no deterrent to attack—attack by the righteous, that is. We might also recall that France and Britain played the crucial role in development of Israel's nuclear arsenal. Imperial sensibilities are delicate indeed.

Had it enjoyed sovereignty, Egypt might have undergone an industrial revolution in the nineteenth century. It shared many of the advantages of the United States, except independence, which allowed the United States to impose very high tariffs to bar superior British goods (textiles, steel, and others). The United States in fact became the world's leader in protectionism until the Second World War, when its economy so overwhelmed anyone else's that "free competition" was tolerable. After the war, massive reliance on the dynamic state sector became a central component of the U.S. economy, even more than it had been before, continuing right to the present. And the United States remains committed to protectionism, when useful. The most extreme protectionism was during the Reagan years—accompanied, as usual, by eloquent odes to liberalism, for others. Reagan virtually doubled protective barriers, and also turned to the usual device, the Pentagon, to overcome management failures and "reindustrialize America," the slogan of the business press. Furthermore, high levels of protectionism are built into the so-called free trade agreements, designed to protect the powerful and privileged, in the traditional manner.

The same was true of Britain's flirtation with "free trade" a century earlier, when 150 years of protectionism and state intervention had made Britain by far the world's most powerful economy, free trade seemed an option, given that the playing field was "tilted" in the right direction, to adapt the familiar metaphor. But the British still hedged their bets. They continued to rely on protected markets, state intervention, and also devices not considered by economic historians. One such market was the world's most spectacular narcotrafficking enterprise, designed to break into the China market, and also producing profits that financed the Royal Navy, the administration of conquered India, and the purchase of U.S. cotton—the fuel of the industrial revolution. U.S. cotton production was also based on radical state intervention: slavery, virtual extermination of the native population, and military conquest—almost half of Mexico, to mention one case relevant to current news. When Britain could no longer compete with Japan, it closed off the empire in 1932, followed by other imperial powers, a crucial part of the background for the Second World War. The truth about free trade and economic development has only a limited resemblance to the doctrines professed.

Throughout modern history, democracy and development have had a common enemy: the loss of sovereignty. In a world of states, it is true that decline of sovereignty entails decline of hope for democracy, and decline in ability to conduct social and economic policy. That in turn harms development, a conclusion well confirmed by centuries of economic history. The work of economic historian M. Shahid Alam is particularly enlightening in this respect. In current terminology, the imposed regimes are called neoliberal, so it is fair to say that the common enemy of democracy and development is neoliberalism. With regard to development, one can debate causality, because the factors in economic growth are so poorly understood. But correlations are reasonably clear. The countries that have most rigorously observed neoliberal principles, as in Latin America and elsewhere, have experienced a sharp deterioration of macroeconomic indicators as compared with earlier years. Those that have ignored the principles, as in East Asia, have enjoyed rapid growth. That neoliberalism harms democracy is understandable. Virtually every feature of the neoliberal package, from privatization to freeing financial flows, undermines democracy for clear and well-known reasons.

The crises we face are real and imminent, and in each case means are available to overcome them. The first step is understanding, then organization and appropriate action. This is the path that has often been followed in the past, bringing about a much better world and leaving a legacy of comparative freedom and privilege, for some at least, which can be the basis for moving on. Failure to do so is almost certain to lead to grim consequences, even the end of biology's only experiment with higher intelligence.

Khiam Prison. Sheikh Nabil Qauq shows inside of a cell to Noam Chomsky. (photo by Carol Chomsky)

3

The Great Soul of Power

Noam Chomsky

On May 9, 2006, Noam Chomsky delivered "The Great Soul of Power" as the Edward Said Memorial Lecture at the American University of Beirut (AUB). Noam Chomsky gave a second lecture at the AUB on May 10, 2006, entitled "Biolinguistic Explorations: Design, Development, Evolution." The text of this second lecture is not included in this volume.

It is a challenging task to select a few themes from the remarkable range of the work and life of Edward Said, whom I was privileged to count as a treasured friend for many years. I will keep to two: the culture of empire, and the responsibility of intellectuals—or from a broader perspective, the culture of dominance generally, and the responsibility of those with sufficient privilege and resources so that if they choose to enter the public arena, we call them "intellectuals."

The phrase "responsibility of intellectuals" conceals a crucial ambiguity: it blurs the distinction between "ought" and "is." In terms of "ought," their responsibility should be exactly the same as that of any decent human being, though greater: privilege confers opportunity, and opportunity confers moral responsibility. We rightly condemn the obedient intellectuals of brutal and violent states for their "conformist subservience to those in power"—I am borrowing the phrase from Hans Morgenthau, one of the founders of modern international relations theory.[1] He was not, however, referring to the commissar class of the totalitarian enemy, but to Western intellectuals, whose crimes are far greater, because they cannot plead fear but only cowardice and subordination to power. He was describing what *is*, not what *ought* to be. And regrettably, he is basically correct about what *is*, and has been throughout much of history. It is noteworthy that he was writing in late 1970, after opposition to the Indochina wars had peaked, and at the time of the most vocal dissidence of the educated classes.

The history of intellectuals is written by intellectuals, so not surprisingly, they are portrayed as defenders of right and justice, upholding the highest values and confronting power and evil with admirable courage and integrity. The record reveals a rather different picture. The term "intellectual" came into common use with the Dreyfusards, the prototypical "engaged intellectuals." But they were a minority: most kept to conformist subservience to those in power. That has been the pattern back to the earliest recorded history. It was the man who "corrupted the youth of Athens" with "false gods" who drank the hemlock, not those who worshipped the true gods of the doctrinal system. A large part of the Bible is devoted to people who provided critical geopolitical analysis and condemned the crimes of state and immoral practices. They are called "prophets," a dubious translation of an obscure word. In contemporary terms, they can be called "dissident intellectuals." There is no need to review how they were treated: miserably, the norm for dissidents.

There were also intellectuals who were greatly respected in the era of the prophets: the flatterers at the court. Centuries later they were condemned as "false prophets." The Gospels warn of "false prophets, who come to you in sheep's clothing, but inwardly are ravening wolves. By their fruits ye shall know them." That's correct: it is by their acts, not their lofty words, that we should know them, a good lesson to the present day.

The end of the last millennium was surely one of the low points in the generally dismal history of intellectuals. In the United States and Europe, respected figures were entranced by the "normative revolution" unfolding before our eyes, as U.S. foreign policy entered a "noble phase" with a "saintly glow." For the first time in history, a state was dedicated to "principles and values," acting from "altruism" alone. At last the "enlightened states" would undertake their "responsibility to protect" the suffering everywhere, led by the "idealistic New World bent on ending inhumanity."[2] That is a small sample from the left-liberal end of the deluge, and deluge it was. The illustrations offered collapse under the slightest examination, and while the chorus of self-adulation was resounding, the idealistic New World and its European allies were conducting some of the most horrendous atrocities of those ugly years. But none of that matters in a well-disciplined intellectual culture, and those who dare sully the record with boring facts can quickly be dismissed as "anti-Americans," if not worse, as Edward Said knew well.

The jewel in the crown was the bombing of Serbia in 1999. Standard doctrine—to quote one respected source—is that NATO went to war "to stop the ethnic cleansing ordered by" Miloševic against Kosovar Albanians, and the U.S.-led campaign "succeeded in stopping the violence."[3] Close to 100 percent of the flood of commentary on the war repeats this story, reversing the chronology: the ethnic cleansing was the consequence of the NATO bombing, not its cause, and furthermore its anticipated consequence. The Miloševic indictment, issued at the height of the bombing on the basis of U.S. and UK intelligence, refers only to crimes after the bombing, with a single exception that occurred two months earlier. The truth of the matter is demonstrated conclusively by a vast collection of detailed documents from the most impeccable sources: the U.S. State Department, the OSCE (Organization for Security and Cooperation in Europe), NATO, the British Parliament, and others, all in full agreement that the atrocities followed the bombing, and admittedly were its anticipated consequence. The same documentary record shows that the pre-bombing period was ugly, though regrettably not in the least unusual, and not even close to the crimes that the United States and United Kingdom were implementing at the same time. According to the British government, until shortly before the NATO bombing most of the atrocities were committed by Kosovo Liberation Army (KLA) guerrillas attacking from across the border in an effort to elicit a harsh Serbian reaction, which could be used to bring about Western intervention. And the Western documentation reveals that nothing changed up until the onset of the bombing, after which the anticipated atrocities did take place, in reaction.

There is much more, but what is interesting is the desperation to which the Western intellectual classes cling to the reversal of chronology and a flood of other lies about what happened. The single example I quoted illustrating the deluge is particularly interesting. It appears in *Political Science Quarterly*, in a laudatory review of John Norris's *Collision Course: NATO, Russia, and Kosovo*, a book that draws precisely the opposite conclusion, and from a highly authoritative source: the highest level of the Clinton administration. John Norris concludes, articulating the thinking of administration planners, that "it was Yugoslavia's resistance to the broader trends of political and economic reform—not the plight of Kosovar Albanians—that best explains NATO's war."[4] As the words pass through the distorting prism of the intellectual culture, these conclusions are transmuted to the doctrine required for the chorus of self-adulation: NATO went to war "to stop the ethnic cleansing ordered by" Miloševic against Kosovar Albanians, and the U.S.-

led campaign "succeeded in stopping the violence." There is virtually nothing that can shake the dogmas required to uphold the nobility of state power, despite the occasional errors and failures that critics allow themselves to condemn.

The grip of imperial culture is sometimes utterly astounding. Even calls for genocide from the highest level of government elicit hardly a murmur. The prosecutors at The Hague were working hard to establish a charge of genocide against Milošević. Suppose they had come across a document in which he orders the Serbian armed forces to carry out a "massive bombing campaign. . . . Anything that flies on anything that moves."[5] The trial would have been over, and Milošević sentenced to life imprisonment, if not worse. Actually they did find such a document, but from the wrong source: Henry Kissinger, conveying orders from the President to bomb Cambodia. I have never found such an explicit call for genocide in the archival record of any state. It was published in the *New York Times* two years ago, eliciting not a murmur of protest, not even qualms. And as educated readers knew, the orders were implemented—though they could not have known how awesome was the scale, because that was kept quiet. Newly released Pentagon records, still unreported, reveal that the bombing of Cambodia was about five times the scale of the horrifying figures that were previously announced: close to three million tons of bombs, nearly half of all U.S. bombings of Indochina, making Cambodia the most heavily bombed country in history, by a wide margin.

All of this happens to be highly relevant to today's crises. The order for genocide in Cambodia was part of the last stages of the Vietnam War, when U.S. troops were being withdrawn to be replaced by airpower, just what is now being planned in Iraq.

The ability "not to see" what might conflict with the image of righteousness often reaches impressive heights. To mention another current example, last February the *New York Times* published an article by law professor Noah Feldman, who failed to impose a U.S.-written constitution on Iraq, which was part of the effort to ensure that the wrong people would not be elected, as he explained. Feldman was reviewing a collection of speeches of Osama bin Laden, and described his descent to greater and greater evil, finally reaching the absolute lowest depths, when he came to advocate "the perverse claim that since the United States is a democracy, all citizens bear responsibility for their government's actions, and civilians are therefore fair targets."[6] The ultimate evil.

Two days later, the lead article in the *New York Times* announced that the United States and Israel were adopting Osama's "perverse claim," joining him in the lower depths of evil. The article reports that Palestinians bear responsibility for their government, so all must suffer for electing Hamas. They will be held hostage and punished until they elect a government favored by the imperial overlords. Detailed mechanisms are outlined, and have since been implemented. The article also reports that Condoleezza Rice will visit the oil producers to ensure that they do not relieve the torture of the Palestinians. When we adopt Osama's perverse principle, it is not ultimate evil, but has different names, like "promoting democracy" and the noble pursuit of peace and justice.

All of this passed without notice: crucially, the fact that Osama's perverse doctrine has been U.S.-UK policy as far back as we would like to go. Well-known cases include "making the economy scream" in Chile, when citizens of Latin America's oldest democracy elected the wrong person. That was the "soft track"; the "hard track" led to the imposition of the Pinochet regime on the first 9/11, as South Americans call it: September 11, 1973, far more hideous than the second one in 2001. Or to take a more recent example, Afghanistan, where after three weeks of bombing, the United States and United Kingdom announced a new war aim: to overthrow the Taliban. Admiral Sir Michael Boyce, chief of the British Defence Staff, announced that U.S.-UK bombing will continue "until the people of the country themselves recognize that this is going to go on until they get the leadership changed," a particularly extreme version of Osama's "perverse claim" because the attackers were well aware that millions of people faced possible death from starvation if the bombing continued.[7] We may also recall the murderous U.S.-UK sanctions against Iraq, killing hundreds of thousands of people and shattering the society, while "paralyzing all opposition to the discredited and moribund regime and giving it a new lease on life," Iraqi dissident Kamil Mahdi wrote.[8]

We also have to forget the most venerable current example: Cuba. Washington has been running campaigns of terror and economic strangulation against Cuba for over forty-five years. The reasons are frankly explained in the secret internal record, from the start: the Eisenhower administration determined that "the Cuban people [are] responsible for the regime," so the United States has the right to cause them to suffer by economic strangulation. "Rising discomfort among hungry Cubans" will cause them to throw Castro out, President Kennedy advised, while also initiating a massive terror campaign that almost brought the world to destruction at the Cuban missile crisis. "Every possible means should be undertaken promptly to weaken the economic life of Cuba [in order to] bring about hunger, desperation and [the] overthrow of the government," the State Department advised.[9] The basic thinking has not changed since. After the collapse of the Soviet Union, Clinton Democrats used Cuba's desperate straits to tighten the vise, intensifying the blockade with the announced objective "to wreak havoc in Cuba," so that the people will suffer and overthrow the government—targeted for attack because of its "successful defiance" of U.S. policies going back to the Monroe Doctrine 180 years ago, we learn from records of the Kennedy-Johnson years.

Adopting Osama's most perverse claim to punish Palestinians is no departure from the routine. But thanks to a good education, none of this can be perceived, even when the articles denouncing Osama and lauding ourselves for joining him in the depths of evil appear simultaneously. Such illustrations, easily multiplied, are real triumphs of imperial culture, fully shared in Europe.

Though the end-of-millennium chorus of self-adulation may well have set a new low in the annals of intellectual history, the norm is not very different. U.S. president John Adams expressed the prevailing truth two centuries ago: "Power always thinks it has a great soul and vast views beyond the comprehension of the weak."[10] That is the deep root of the combination of savagery and self-righteousness that infects the imperial mentality—and in some measure, every structure of authority and domination.

Reverence for that great soul is the normal stance of intellectual elites, who regularly add that they should hold the levers of control, or at least be close by. That doctrine holds across the narrow spectrum: it is the standard Leninist doctrine, shared by progressive thought in the West: the so-called action intellectuals of Kennedy's Camelot, for example. The leading public intellectual of twentieth-century America, the Wilsonian political analyst Walter Lippmann, explained in his essays on democracy that the "responsible" intellectuals who design and implement policy must "live free of the trampling and roar of [the] bewildered herd," as they labor selflessly for the common good, while the herd must be "put in its place": attending to private pursuits.[11] One common expression of this prevailing view is that there are two categories of intellectuals: the "technocratic and policy-oriented intellectuals"—responsible, sober, constructive—and the "value-oriented intellectuals," a sinister grouping who pose a threat to democracy as they "devote themselves to the derogation of leadership, the challenging of authority, and the unmasking of established institutions," even seeking to delegitimate the institutions responsible for the "indoctrination of the young": the schools, colleges, churches, and so on.[12] I am quoting from a study by the more progressive and humane wing of the international intellectual class—the liberal internationalists of the Trilateral Commission, from the United States, Europe, and Japan. The Carter administration was almost entirely drawn from their ranks, including the president. They were reflecting on the "crisis of democracy" that developed in the 1960s, when normally passive and apathetic sectors of the population, called "the special interests," sought to enter the political arena to advance their concerns. Those improper initiatives created what they called a crisis of democracy, in which the proper functioning of the state was threatened by "excessive democracy." To overcome the crisis, the special interests must be restored to their proper function as passive observers, so that the "technocratic and value-oriented intellectuals" can do their constructive work, undisturbed by the bewildered herd.

The disruptive special interests are women, the young, the elderly, workers, farmers, minorities, majorities—in short, the population. Only one specific interest is not mentioned in the study: the corporate sector. But that makes sense. They represent the "national interest," and naturally there can be no question of the national interest being protected by state power. I stress again that I am quoting from the liberal internationalist extreme of the spectrum. The business world and the right took a much harsher stand, and implemented their decisions so as to beat back the dangerous civilizing and democratizing tide, with some success. Those reactions have set their stamp on the contemporary era, in a wide variety of ways, ranging from doctrinal management to global economic policies.

There have always been radical extremists who reject the prevailing premises. Some of them, centuries ago, went so far as to condemn the "merchants and manufacturers" who were the "principal architects of policy" in England, and used their power to make sure that their own interests were "most peculiarly attended to," no matter how "grievous" the impact on others, primarily those in India and elsewhere who were subject to their "savage injustice," but also the population at home. According to these renegades, a primary task of the ruling economic class is to "delude and oppress the public," as they pursue the "vile maxim of the masters of mankind: all for ourselves, nothing for other people." Such radical extremists are either ignored or reviled. In the case of Adam Smith, whom I am quoting, ignored. He is revered, but unread; his leading ideas are not only ignored but often simply falsified. To mention only one case of unusual contemporary relevance, everyone has heard his phrase "invisible hand," but few have taken the trouble to find the phrase in his classic *Wealth of Nations*. It appears just once, in an argument against what is now called "neoliberalism." Neoliberal principles, Smith recognized, would devastate England if the merchants and manufacturers who ruled the state in their own interest would invest abroad and rely on imports. But they will not do so, Smith suggested, because they prefer to do business at home, so as if by an invisible hand, England will be saved from the ravages of neoliberalism. David Ricardo made similar observations, adding "these feelings, which I should be sorry to see weakened, induce most men of property to be satisfied with a low rate of profits in their own country, rather than seek a more advantageous employment for their wealth in foreign nations," in which case his theory of comparative advantage would collapse.[13]

England, of course, did not rely on the invisible hand to ensure that it would develop. England relied on a powerful interventionist state, while its colonies were crushed by forceful imposition of free trade. The merchants and manufacturers who ruled England were unwilling even to toy with the idea of free trade until 1846, after 150 years of protectionism and violence had created far and away the most powerful industrial society in the world. They could therefore expect that the "playing field would be tilted" in their favor, to adopt the contemporary idiom, so that "free competition" would be acceptable. But they were careful to hedge their bets. They relied crucially on their protected markets in India and elsewhere, while also developing the most extraordinary narcotrafficking enterprise in human history to enable them to break into the China market. The United States followed the same path, as have other countries that have developed, in radical violation of the precepts of economic theory, again a pattern that persists to the present. But that is another topic.

For those who want to understand today's world and what is likely to lie ahead, it is of prime importance to look closely at the long-standing principles that are held to animate the decisions and actions of the powerful—bearing in mind that it is by their fruits that you shall know them, not their fine words. In today's world, that means primarily the United States. Though only one of three major power centers in economic and most other dimensions, it surpasses any power in history in its military dominance, which is rapidly expanding, and it can generally rely on the support of the second superpower, Europe, and also Japan, the second-largest industrial economy. There is a clear doctrine on the general contours of U.S. foreign policy. It reigns virtually without exception in Western journalism and almost all scholarship, even among critics of policies past and present. The major theme is "American exceptionalism": the thesis that the United States is unlike other great powers, past and present, because it has a "transcendent purpose": "the establishment of equality in freedom in America," and indeed throughout the world, since "the arena within which the United States must defend and promote its purpose has become world-wide."[14]

Hans Morgenthau's exposition of the "transcendent purpose" is in his book *The Purpose of American Politics*, written during the Kennedy years, after the Vietnam War, in another period of extreme self-adulation among responsible intellectuals. Morgenthau was the founder of the dominant tough-minded *realist* school of international affairs, which avoids sentimentality and keeps to the hard truths of state power. He was incidentally a very decent human being: he was one of the few prominent scholars in these fields to oppose the Vietnam War on moral grounds, not on grounds of cost-effectiveness, a stance that was extremely rare in intellectual circles, though not among the unwashed masses. By 1969, 70 percent of the U.S. public condemned the war as "not a mistake," but "fundamentally wrong and immoral."[15] These are words rarely heard within the mainstream, across the spectrum.

Morgenthau was also a highly competent and honest scholar. While praising the transcendent purpose of America, he recognized that the historical record is radically inconsistent with it. But he explains that we should not be misled by that discrepancy. In his words, we should not "confound the abuse of reality with reality itself." Reality is the unachieved "national purpose" revealed by "the evidence of history as our minds reflect it." The actual historical record is merely the "abuse of reality," which is of only secondary interest—at least to those who are holding the clubs.[16]

The principles continue to guide intellectual practice, including most scholarship. Just keeping to the present, the most extensive scholarly article on "the roots of the Bush doctrine" appears in the prestigious U.S. journal *International Security*. Jonathan Morton opens this article with these words: "The promotion of democracy is central to the George W. Bush administration's prosecution of both the war on terrorism and its overall grand strategy."[17] In Britain's leading journal of international affairs, Katerina Dalacoura extends the scope of the thesis. She writes that "promoting democracy abroad" has been a primary goal ever since Woodrow Wilson endowed U.S. foreign policy with a "powerful idealist element," which gained "particular salience" under Reagan and has been taken up with "unprecedented forcefulness" under George W. Bush.[18] Such declarations are close to uniform in scholarship. In journalism and intellectual commentary, they are taken to be the merest truisms. To be sure, there are critics who argue that it is important not to go too far in our idealism, because it can be harmful to our interests. To take one significant example, David Ignatius, the veteran commentator of the *Washington Post* and former editor of the *International Herald Tribune*, warns that the "idealist-in-chief" of the Bush administration might be "too idealistic—that his passion for the noble goals of the Iraq war might overwhelm the prudence and pragmatism that normally guide war planners."[19] He was referring to Paul Wolfowitz, who briefly pursued his passion for democracy and development as head of the World Bank. The many accolades to Wolfowitz at the time of his appointment scrupulously evaded his record, which is one of utter contempt for democracy and human rights, easily documented—but abuse of history, hence irrelevant.

The scholarly and journalistic presentation of the reigning thesis also carefully evades empirical evidence, a wise decision, because it is overwhelmingly to the contrary. That is obliquely recognized in serious scholarship that focuses specifically on democracy promotion—Bush's "messianic mission," as it is described in the liberal press. The most prominent scholar-advocate of the cause of democracy promotion is Thomas Carothers, director of the Democracy and Rule of Law Project at the Carnegie Endowment. He identifies himself as a neo-Reaganite, agreeing with general scholarship that Wilsonian idealism took on particular "salience" under Reagan's leadership. A year after the invasion of Iraq, he published *Critical Mission*, a book reviewing the record of democracy promotion by the United States since the end of the Cold War. He finds what he calls "a strong line of continuity" running through Bush I's, Clinton's, and Bush II's administrations: democracy is promoted by the U.S. government *if and only if* it conforms to strategic and economic interests.[20] All administrations are "schizophrenic" in this regard, with puzzling consistency. Again, actual history is the abuse of reality, so it can be ignored in responsible circles.

Carothers also wrote the standard scholarly work on democracy promotion in Latin America in the 1980s from an insider's perspective. He was serving in the Reagan-era State Department, in the programs of democracy promotion. Carothers regards these programs as sincere, but a failure. Like Morgenthau, he is an honest scholar, and points out that the failure of the programs was systematic. Where U.S. influence was least, in South America, progress towards democracy was greatest, despite Reagan's attempts to impede it by embracing right-wing dictators. Where U.S. influence was strongest, in the regions nearby, progress was least. The reasons, he explains, are that Washington would tolerate only "limited, top-down forms of democratic change that did not risk upsetting the traditional structures of power with which the United States has long been allied [in] quite undemocratic societies."[21]

In short, the strong line of continuity goes back a decade earlier, to the Reagan years, when the "powerful idealist element" in traditional U.S. policy gained "particular salience," according to Western scholarship. Nonetheless, the dedication of our leaders to the principle is beyond question, and today we must believe that Bush is pursuing his messianic vision of creating a sovereign, democratic Iraq and bringing democracy everywhere, ignoring the overwhelming consistency of the record: the abuse of history. I am surprised to see the doctrine echoed even in the Arab world, where people surely should know better.

In fact, the strong line of continuity goes back much farther. Democracy promotion has always been proclaimed as a guiding vision, but it is not even controversial that the United States regularly overthrew parliamentary democracies, often installing or supporting brutal tyrannies: Iran, Guatemala, Brazil, Chile, and a long list of others. There were Cold War pretexts, but they regularly collapse on investigation. I will not insult your intelligence by recounting how Reagan brought democracy to Central America in the course of the "war on terror" that the Reagan administration declared when it took office in 1981—quickly becoming an extraordinary terrorist war that left hundreds of thousands of corpses in Central America and four countries in ruins.

The paradoxical character of policy is also recognized at the dovish extreme of the policy spectrum, where it elicits regret, but is recognized to be unavoidable. The basic dilemma facing policymakers was expressed by Robert Pastor, a progressive Latin America scholar and President Carter's national security advisor for Latin America. He explains why the administration had to support the murderous and corrupt Somoza regime in Nicaragua, and when that proved impossible, to try at least to maintain the U.S.-trained National Guard even as it was massacring the population "with a brutality a nation usually reserves for its enemy," killing some 40,000 people. The reason was the familiar one: "The United States did not want to control Nicaragua or the other nations of the region," he writes, "but it also did not want developments to get out of control. It wanted Nicaraguans to act independently, *except* when doing so would affect U.S. interests adversely."[22]

Once again we find the dominant operative principle, illustrated copiously throughout history: policy conforms to expressed ideals only if it also conforms to interests. The term "interests" does not refer to the interests of the domestic U.S. population, but the "national interest"—the interests of the concentrations of power that dominate the domestic society. That truism is often derided by respectable opinion as a "conspiracy theory," or "Marxist," or some other epithet, but it is readily confirmed when subjected to inquiry. In a rare and unusually careful analysis of the domestic influences on U.S. foreign policy, Lawrence R. Jacob and Benjamin I. Page, two prominent political scientists, find, unsurprisingly, that the major influence on policy is "internationally oriented business corporations," though there is also a secondary effect of "experts," who, they point out, "may themselves be influenced by business." In contrast, they find public opinion has "little or no significant effect on government officials." As they note, the results should be welcome to "realists" such as the influential progressive public intellectual Walter Lippmann, who "considered public opinion to be ill-informed and capricious" and "warned that following public opinion would create a 'morbid derangement of the true functions of power' and produce policies 'deadly to the very survival of the state as a free society.' "[23] The "realism" is a scarcely concealed ideological preference. One will search in vain for evidence of the superior understanding and abilities of those who have the major influence on policy, apart from protecting their own interests, Adam Smith's neglected truism.

I will not tarry on how Wilsonian idealism and love of democracy was actually exercised, with devastating effects that remain until today, particularly in Haiti. Once the richest colony in the world and the source of much of France's wealth, Haiti is now decaying in misery and is likely to become uninhabitable before too long, thanks to French brutality and avarice, carried a long step forward by Wilsonian idealism, then its successors through Clinton and Bush. And that is far from the only case. We may recall that Wilson's high-minded passion for self-determination had a qualification: it did not apply to people "at a low stage of civilization," he explained, as in the Middle East, where these defective creatures must be given "friendly protection, guidance, and assistance" by the colonial powers that had tended to their needs in past years, in his words. Wilson's famous Fourteen Points held that in questions of sovereignty, "the interests of the populations concerned must have equal weight with the equitable claims of the government whose title is to be determined," that of the colonial ruler.[24] Posturing aside, Wilson scarcely departed from Churchill's doctrine after the Second World War, when the latter advised: "the government of the world must be entrusted to satisfied nations, who wished nothing more for themselves than what they had. If the world-government were in the hands of hungry nations, there would always be danger. But none of us had any reason to seek for anything more. The peace would be kept by peoples who lived in their own way and were not ambitious. Our power placed us above the rest. We were like rich men dwelling at peace within their habitations."[25]

No sentimentalist, Churchill knew well how Britain's wealth and peace had been obtained. Speaking in secret to his cabinet colleagues on the eve of the First World War, Churchill explained: "We are not a young people with *an innocent record* and a scanty inheritance. We have engrossed to ourselves...an *altogether disproportionate* share of the wealth and traffic of the world. We have got all we want in territory, and our claim to be left in the unmolested enjoyment of vast and splendid possessions, *mainly acquired by violence, largely maintained by force,* often seems less reasonable to others than to us."[26]

Churchill did publish these remarks a decade later, but made sure to delete the offending passages (italicized above), only discovered fairly recently.

Churchill's sensible and realistic stance illustrates one of the many reasons for regarding the fabled "American exceptionalism" with some skepticism. The doctrine appears to be close to a historical universal, even including the worst monsters. Aggression and terror are almost invariably portrayed as self-defense and dedication to inspiring visions. Japanese emperor Hirohito was merely repeating a broken record in his surrender declaration in August 1945, when he told his people that "We declared war on America and Britain out of Our sincere desire to ensure Japan's self-preservation and the stabilization of East Asia, it being far from Our thought either to infringe upon the sovereignty of other nations or to embark upon territorial aggrandizement."[27] If Asians have a different picture, it shows that they are backward and uncivilized people—a leading source of tension in Asia right now. From Japan's perspective, Asians who worry about such ancient history as the Nanjing massacre, biological warfare, and other atrocities are "naughty children who are exercising all the privileges and rights of grown ups" and require "a stiff hand, an authoritative hand," to quote the description of Latin Americans by Secretary of State John Foster Dulles, though he advised President Eisenhower that to control the naughty children more effectively, it may be useful to "pat them a little bit and make them think that you are fond of them."[28]

That stance extends worldwide, and has recently been announced with regard to China. A few weeks ago, as President Hu Jintao was about to visit Washington, the respected commentator Frederick Kempe explained in the *Wall Street Journal* that "Americans aim to show Hu how his country can act as a 'responsible stakeholder,' " joining the United States and its allies in adherence to international law, principles of world order, and civilized behavior.[29] The stance and commentary elicit no ridicule, just as Western intellectuals soberly observe the demand of the United States and United Kingdom that Iran end its interference in Iraq—rather like Hitler's condemnation of U.S.-UK interference in peaceful occupied Europe. Though the matter passed without notice in the media, we can be confident that shivers went up the spines of Washington planners when President Hu left Washington for Saudi Arabia, returning King Abdullah's visit to Beijing. And they surely watch with trepidation as Saudi Arabia has become China's largest trade partner in West Asia and North Africa with bilateral trade reaching $16 billion in 2005 and growing; also in Washington's own backyard in Latin America, regarded previously as a reliable source of oil and other resources, no longer.

While the law-abiding states of the West seek to civilize China, John Steinbruner and Nancy Gallagher—two of the most respected strategic analysts—are calling on China to lead a coalition of peace-loving states to counter U.S. aggressive militarism, which they warn is driving the world towards "ultimate doom." They appeal to China because of all the nuclear powers it "has maintained by far the most restrained pattern of military deployment."[30] China has also led the efforts at the United Nations to block the unilateral U.S. refusal, since the Clinton years, to preserve space for peaceful purposes, now extended by the Bush administration to the doctrine of "ownership of space," leaving every corner of the world subject to near-instantaneous lethal attack without the need for military bases. It is well understood that these moves, which are already eliciting the anticipated reaction among potential targets, pose a severe threat to the survival of the species. Nevertheless, it is China that is to be portrayed to the public as another of those "naughty children" to whom we must teach manners.

The universal stance of "exceptionalism" extends even to the figures of the highest intelligence and moral integrity. Consider John Stuart Mill, who wrote the classic essay on humanitarian intervention, and presumably studied in every serious law school in the West. His essay raised the question of whether England should intervene in the ugly world, or whether it should keep to its own business and let the barbarians carry out their savagery. His conclusion, nuanced and complex, was that England *should* intervene, even though by doing so, it will endure the "obloquy" and abuse of Europeans, who will "seek base motives" because they cannot comprehend that England is a "novelty in the world," an angelic power that seeks nothing for itself and acts only for the benefit of others. Though England selflessly bears the cost of intervention, it shares the benefits of its labors with others equally. Mill's immediate concern was India. He was calling for the expansion of the occupation of India to several new provinces.

The timing of the article is revealing. The essay appeared in 1859, immediately after what British history calls the "Indian mutiny": the first rebellion in India, which Britain put down with extreme savagery. All of this was very well known in England. There were parliamentary debates and a huge controversy. There were people who opposed the crimes: Richard Cobden, a committed liberal in the old-fashioned sense, and a few others. Mill was corresponding secretary of the East India Company and was following it all closely. The purpose of the expansion of British power over India was to obtain a monopoly over opium so that England could break into the Chinese market, which British exporters could not penetrate because Chinese goods were comparable and they didn't want British goods. So the only way to sell to them was to force the Chinese to become a nation of opium addicts at the point of a gun. Mill was writing right at the time of the Second Opium War, which established Britain's extraordinary narcotrafficking enterprise, which I already mentioned, and did enable England, and later others, to subjugate China and break into its markets. The profits were an enormous boost to British capitalism, right during the period of much pious rhetoric about free trade. In the same essay, Mill also praised the civilizing mission of the French, then underway in North Africa under the orders of the French Minister of War, who called for "exterminating the indigenous population," with little dissent among the engaged intellectuals.[31]

Exceptionalism seems to be close to universal. I suspect if we had records from Genghis Khan, we might find the same thing. Nonetheless, it is the responsibility of intellectuals to recognize the doctrine as a driving force of U.S. policy, even if they sometimes criticize the idealism as excessive—as in the case of the "idealist-in-chief" in charge of the "noble war" in Iraq.

The great soul of power extends far beyond states. Slavery was defended with arguments similar to those of Mill: it was a selfless exercise of benevolence to poor people who needed the care of their masters, and if they were "naughty children," they sometimes needed the rod, or worse, for their own benefit. Some of the arguments of the slave-owners were never really countered. To rephrase anachronistically, suppose I buy a car and you rent one. A year later, which one is likely to be in better shape? Mine, surely, because I protect my capital investment, while you can discard yours and rent another one. Suppose now that I own workers and you rent them. Who is more benign? That argument had considerable force for working people who fought for the Union in the American Civil War, under the banner that wage slavery is little different from chattel slavery, and that it is an attack on fundamental human rights to reduce people to the level where they must rent themselves to survive—a perception so common that it was even a slogan of the Republican Party. That was 150 years ago to be sure; we have become more civilized since, and are not supposed to see such social-economic arrangements as an attack on the most fundamental human rights.

The great soul of power extends to every domain of life, from families to international affairs. And throughout, every form of authority and domination bears a severe burden of proof. It is not self-legitimating. When it cannot bear the burden, as is commonly the case, it should be dismantled. That has been the guiding theme of the anarchist movements in their modern origins, adopting many of the principles of classical liberalism after it has been wrecked on the shoals of capitalism, as the anarchist historian Rudolf Rocker wrote.[32] Keeping to the international arena, the contemporary system of nation-states was established with extreme violence and sadism, which for centuries made Europe the most savage region of the world, ending in 1945, when it was recognized that the next time Europeans play the game of mutual slaughter will be the last. Eliminate that factor, and the thesis of "democratic peace" that is much prized in political science loses its core empirical support. There is good reason to believe that the culture of savagery that evolved in the course of establishing the state system was a significant factor in Europe's conquest of the world. The inhabitants of Asia and the Western Hemisphere were "appalled by the all-destructive fury of European warfare," military historian Geoffrey Parker observes, enabling "the white peoples of the world...to create and control" history's "first global hegemony."[33] British historian V. G. Kiernan aptly comments that "Europe's incessant wars" were responsible for "stimulating military science and spirit to a point where Europe would be crushingly superior to the rest when they did meet."[34] Imposition of the European-style state system on the conquered lands was carried out with comparable brutality, and lies at the root of indescribable horrors, including the conflicts that rage today.

One of the most healthy recent developments in Europe, along with the federal arrangements and increased fluidity that the European Union has brought, is the devolution of state power, along with revival of traditional cultures and languages and a degree of regional autonomy. These developments lead some to envision a future Europe of the regions, with state authority decentralized. No one wants to reconstruct the Ottoman empire, with its brutality and corruption, but that should not prevent us from recognizing that in some respects it had the right idea: leaving people alone to manage their own affairs, without strict borders and with substantial peaceful interaction at local and regional levels, a conception that should have particular resonance, and memories, in the complex societies of the Levant, and has merits far beyond. To strike a proper balance between citizenship and common purpose on the one hand, and communal autonomy and cultural variety on the other, is no simple matter, and questions of democratic control of institutions of course extend to other spheres of life as well. Such questions should be high on the agenda of people who do not worship at the shrine of the great soul of power, people who seek to save the world from the destructive forces that now literally threaten survival and who believe that a more civilized society can be envisioned and even brought into existence—the cause to which Edward devoted his life and work.

Khiam Prison. Noam Chomsky, Sheikh Nabil Qauq (left), and Assaf Kfoury (center) look at commemorative photo of resistance fighters celebrating withdrawal of Israeli troops in May 2000. (photo by Carol Chomsky)

4

U.S. Foreign Policy and the Middle East: An Interview with Noam Chomsky

Noam Chomsky Interviewed by Marcel Ghanem

Noam Chomsky participated in a televised interview with Marcel Ghanem of the Lebanese Broadcasting Corporation (LBC) on May 14, 2006. The interview was broadcast on May 19. Marcel Ghanem is the host of a popular political talk show on LBC, Kalam al-Nass *("*Talk of the People*"), with a large following in Lebanon and other Arab countries. Below is a transcription of this interview.*

Marcel Ghanem: Good evening and welcome, Professor Noam Chomsky. Thank you for agreeing to an exclusive interview here on *Kalam al-Nass.* The *New York Times* calls Professor Chomsky an "international phenomenon" and one of the most widely read authors on issues of U.S. foreign policy. In a survey, he was voted one of the ten most influential personalities in the second half of the twentieth century.

Professor Chomsky, which has affected you more: the opinion of the *New York Times* or that of David Horowitz, the former leftist turned neoconservative, who has called you a "sick mind"?

Noam Chomsky: Actually, neither affected me in the least, so I can't say which affected me more. I don't pay much attention to the opinions of those who serve power.

MG: A key date in the recent history of Lebanon is March 14, 2005, also known as the Cedar Revolution. What will be the next stage? The Lebanon of the Cedar

Revolution or the Lebanon of Hezbollah? Did you find out when you were there what Lebanon needs most?

NC: Lebanon has obviously a complex, intricate society with many different aspects to it. I knew that before I came. I have been acquainted with the history of Lebanon for many years. I have written about it. It is different to see Lebanon firsthand, but I think the split into Cedar Revolution or Hezbollah is a bit artificial. I think there is a general consensus that Syria should not occupy and control Lebanon. That is, I think, accepted by most, and insofar as the Cedar Revolution succeeded to a large degree in removing Syrian control, that is a good thing. It is thirty years late in my opinion, but it happened. Hezbollah is part of Lebanese society, it represents a substantial segment of it, but it has positions that are not shared by others. These are internal problems, which must be solved internally. Lebanese society is split along different lines—confessional lines, class lines, and many others.

MG: The U.S. administration says that Hezbollah is a terrorist organization. Don't you agree?

NC: The United States considers Hezbollah a terrorist organization, but the term "terrorism" is used by powerful nations for forms of violence they disapprove of. The United States supported the Israeli invasion and occupation of southern Lebanon. Hezbollah was instrumental in driving them out, therefore they are a terrorist organization.

MG: Professor Chomsky, in your latest book you discuss the topic of failed states. One of the characteristics of these states is the inability of their government to control all the land. According to this definition, is Lebanon a "failed state"?

NC: Lebanon has innumerable problems. Failed states are defined by several distinct symptoms. One such symptom is that the state is unwilling or unable to protect the security and well-being of its citizens—this is a primary feature of a failed state. I should say that by this criterion one of the leading failed states in the world is the United States. It is consciously increasing the threat to its own citizens, the threat of terror, and the threat of terminal nuclear war, of global disaster. For example, the invasion of Iraq, undertaken with the knowledge that it could trigger an escalation of terrorist activity, may increase the threat of nuclear proliferation and hence lead to the very serious possibility of a nuclear war. That is one characteristic of a failed state. I should say that in this respect the state of Lebanon, which is a weak state in terms of its national institutions, has also been unable to protect the security and well-being of its citizens. I need not talk about that. Furthermore, a failed state may have democratic institutions, formal democratic institutions, but they have only limited capacities and do not function effectively. We can say that the United States and Lebanon, in different respects, share this characteristic of failed states. There are other characteristics that are shared by powerful and weak states.

MG: There are different theories in Lebanon regarding our role in the region and in the Arab-Israeli conflict. After thirty years of war, will Lebanon be allowed to assume a more neutral position in the Arab-Israeli conflict and to concentrate on the construction of a modern state?

NC: Lebanon has been a victim of the Arab-Israeli conflict without participating in it directly. It was the victim of the 1948 war, when hundreds of thousands of Palestinians were expelled or fled from Israel. The same happened again during and after the 1967 war. Lebanon has been repeatedly invaded. Four invasions since 1978 from the south; U.S.-backed Israeli invasions. Bombing and terror. The Palestinian refugees have participated in Lebanon's complex political conflicts and in the civil war. In all of these aspects, Lebanon was and is the victim of the Arab-Israeli conflict, and it will remain so until that conflict is resolved. There will be internal problems in Lebanon, and the future of the Palestinian population in Lebanon is an open question. Lebanon and the rest of the world must solve this question one way or another. It is of course connected to a settlement of the Arab-Israeli conflict over the lands of the former Palestine.

MG: Moving to the subject of Palestine, Professor Chomsky, do you agree with the demand that the Palestinian refugees abandon their right of return? You are a supporter of the Geneva Agreement from December 2003, which does not oblige Israel to accept the return of Palestinian refugees.

NC: There was a tentative agreement regarding Israel and the Palestinian refugees. It was almost finalized in Taba in January 2001. The Palestinian Authority and the Israeli government had extensive meetings there within the framework that was called "President Clinton's parameters." These were proposed after the collapse of the Camp David negotiations. President Clinton recognized that the proposals made at Camp David were unacceptable. In December 2000, he offered a modified version, the so-called parameters. Israel and the Palestinians continued to negotiate within this framework, and they came close to a resolution. According to participants on both sides, had the Taba negotiations continued they might well have resolved the problem, at least temporarily. The negotiations were called off by Israel. They brought no results, but they did include a discussion of the refugee problem, and the general agreement was that within the framework of a two-state settlement—roughly on the international border with some land swaps—Israel would permit the return of a certain number of refugees to the State of Israel. Others would return to the Palestinian state, and others would enjoy certain opportunities granted by the international community. The agreement specified that the return of refugees would be on a scale that does not upset the demographic balance in Israel, the Jewish majority, and that Israel would remain a Jewish state. That was the general framework. It was never finalized, but a resolution came within reach. Something along these lines remains feasible. After the breakdown, both sides continued informal negotiations at a relatively high level, which produced a number of results. The most prominent is the Geneva Accord, announced in Geneva in December 2003. It proposes a similar solution of the refugee problem: some would return to Israel, some to Palestine, in a way that would preserve the demographic balance in Israel. But it is an informal agreement that can only be implemented if it is accepted formally by the signatories and by the world. Israel rejected it; so did the United States. The negotiations continue, but only if and when the United States accepts them will they produce concrete results.

MG: There is a reality in Israel and Palestine today: Hamas is in power as a result of democratic elections, and they are an organization that refuses to recognize Israel and is banned by the international community. Israeli Prime Minister Ehud Olmert, in contrast, proposes a plan for unilateral withdrawal and for a unilateral delimitation of borders. Is there a solution to this dilemma?

NC: It is an interesting dilemma. Personally, I am opposed to Hamas's policies in almost every respect. However, we should recognize that the policies of Hamas are more forthcoming and more conducive to a peaceful settlement than those of the United States and Israel. Let me repeat: Hamas's policies are in my view unacceptable, but at the same time preferable to those of the United States and Israel. For example, Hamas has called for a long-term indefinite truce along the international border. There is a long-standing international consensus that goes back over thirty years that there should be a two-state political settlement on the international border. Hamas is willing to accept the pre-June 1967 border with "minor and mutual modifications"—that is the official phrase—as basis for a long-term truce, while the United States and Israel are unwilling to even consider it. The demands on Hamas by the United States, the European Union, and Israel are: first, recognize the State of Israel, or actually, recognize its right to exist. Well, Israel and the United States do not recognize a state of Palestine. In fact, they have consistently undermined any such possibility. The second condition is that Hamas must renounce violence. Yet Israel and the United States do not renounce violence. The third condition is that Hamas accept international agreements. The United States and Israel reject international agreements. (That includes the Road Map of the quartet, constantly brought up in this connection. Israel claimed to accept it, but with fourteen reservations that effectively eliminated its content, with tacit U.S. approval.) So again, even though the policies of Hamas are in my view unacceptable, they happen to be closer to the international consensus on a political peaceful settlement than those of their counterparts. It is a reflection of the power of the imperial states, that is, the United States and Europe, that they are able to shift their framework in such a way that the policies of Hamas appear to be the problem, and not the more extreme ones of the United States and Israel. And remember, this is not just a matter of policies or words, but of concrete actions, the current actions of the United States and Israel. Anything that Israel does has the permission and the support of the United States. They have a joint policy. The policies of the United States and Israel are in effect to annex those portions of the West Bank that they regard as valuable in terms of land and resources, and to essentially imprison Palestinians in separated cantons, surrounded on all sides by territories taken over by Israel. If you look at the territorial borders that are being annexed, they include two corridors that cut right through Palestine. A southern one from East Jerusalem runs all the way to the Jordan Valley, and a second one further north starts east of the Israeli city Ariel, separating the northern part of the West Bank from the central region. East Jerusalem is essentially isolated. That means you end up with four sectors. These are not words, not plans, these are acts which are being undertaken. If we compare the policies of the two sides, they are all unacceptable, but those of Hamas are the least unacceptable. Framing the issue the way it has been done is a reflection of the power of the Western nations. They are able to impose their framework of discussion, and this is not something we should accept.

MG: Let us now turn to U.S. foreign policy. Professor Chomsky, you are considered one of its most prominent critics. To some, it sounds like you have only one message: America is the "great Satan" and the source of evil throughout the world. Is it possible, as David Horowitz has accused you of saying, that America is not only responsible for its own wrongs, but also for those of others, including the 9/11 attacks?

NC: What David Horowitz has to say has about as much interest to me as what the most extreme partisans of the Communist Party in Russia had to say. I paid no attention when I was denounced by the Soviet Union bitterly for years. It is of no interest to me when their counterparts in the United States do the same thing. As far as 9/11 is concerned, I take the position I have expressed in writing immediately after the attacks, a position which I still hold. Until today, it remains one of the most horrifying terrorist atrocities, but we should also recognize that its scale, as far as terrorist acts are concerned, is not unusual. In fact, in Latin America it is often called the second 9/11, because on September 11, 1973, there occurred another terrorist attack that was even worse. September 11, 2001, was bad enough, but let us imagine another course of events: suppose al-Qaeda had succeeded in attacking the White House, killed the President, installed a military dictatorship, a brutal regime killing 50,000 to 100,000 people and torturing 700,000, and set up a worldwide terrorist network that would overthrow governments, carry out assassinations, and so on. Suppose all this would have happened on 9/11. Well, in fact it did, it happened on September 11, 1973, in Chile. I only changed the numbers to get a per capita equivalence. This scenario is much worse than the attack that took place in the United States, and it did happen. The United States backed the installation of a military dictatorship in Chile, which overthrew and destroyed the oldest democratic system in Latin America. This is only one example, there are many others. Yes, September 11, 2001, was a terrible atrocity. In the West it is considered unique, and in a sense this is true. For the first time in hundreds of years massive terrorism has been directed against the West. However, the West is the source of far worse violence and terrorism directed against others. We should recognize what happened on 9/11 as a crime and atrocity and place it in the context of history. Commentators in the United States, of whom David Horowitz is just one example, do not want the situation to be presented this way, just as their counterparts in the Soviet Union did not want actual history to be presented this way.

MG: But the foreign policy of President George W. Bush did achieve results. Most importantly, we did not witness any terrorist attacks on American soil since 9/11. In the eyes of some, your criticism of George Bush is undermining your credibility. First, Afghanistan is no longer a safe harbor for terrorists. The terrorist network there has been isolated. Second, Muammar al-Gaddafi is no longer trying to develop nuclear weapons. And lastly, there were free and open elections in Afghanistan and Iraq. One could also include democratic tendencies in Egypt, and the end of the Syrian occupation of Lebanon. These achievements took place after 9/11. Are they not attributable to the policies of George Bush?

NC: The first achievement of George Bush after 9/11 was to attack Afghanistan. Let us take a look at what happened. The attack was carried out for one explicit reason—the objective of the war was stated explicitly. According to Bush, any state that harbors terrorists is a terrorist state and must be treated accordingly. It must be bombed and invaded. It seems to me that Bush is calling for the bombing of the United States. The United States harbors terrorists who are regarded as such by the FBI and the Justice Department. One of the worst is Orlando Bosch, the anti-Castro terrorist accused of about thirty terrorist acts by the FBI, among them the crash of a Cubana Airline plane killing seventy-three people. This was part of the U.S. terror war against Cuba that lasted forty-five years. Bush's father, George Herbert Walker Bush, gave Bosch a presidential pardon. Bosch remained in the United States against the objections of the Justice Department, which regarded him as a national security threat. I can go on from there to the main terrorists who operate from Washington.

MG: Professor Chomsky, are you a supporter of the Taliban regime?

NC: That is an interesting question, and again, it illustrates the amazing power of Western propaganda. Bush demanded that the Taliban turn over to the United States persons whom the United States suspected of involvement in 9/11—that was the aim of the war. It had nothing to do with the overthrow of the Taliban. The Taliban requested evidence, which Bush refused to supply. We know why. Eight months later, after the most intensive investigation in U.S. history, the FBI informed the press that they suspected that the plans for 9/11 were hatched in Afghanistan, and implemented in Germany and the United Arab Emirates. That was what they suspected after eight months, but they had no clear evidence. Afghanistan was bombed because of suspicions that the United States had, but could not confirm. After three weeks of bombing, the war aim changed. It was announced by the British official in charge. He said something like this: we will continue to bomb the people of Afghanistan until they overthrow their government. That is international terrorism, and a particularly vicious form of it, for Britain and the United States knew from their own estimates that sustained bombing might drive millions into starvation. Many Afghans were barely surviving before the war. This switch occurred three weeks after the bombing began. Now, the story of the invasion of Afghanistan has been rewritten by the Western media, making it sound as if the United States invaded to overthrow a tyrannical regime. That is an illustration of the power of the imperial propaganda systems of the West. But the documentation is plain and simple. Furthermore, I should say that the invasion of Afghanistan was undertaken against enormous public opposition throughout the world. International polls conducted right before the bombing, notably by the Gallup Organization, showed extremely low support for the war. In Europe, except for England, it did not go beyond 25 percent. In Latin America it was almost invisible. To repeat, the cause of the war was the refusal of the Afghan government to turn over to the United States persons whom the United States suspected of involvement in the 9/11 attacks. Three weeks later, the purpose of the war was changed to bombing the people of Afghanistan until they overthrow their government. This is a textbook example of international terrorism on a vast scale. I should also mention that the bombing was strongly opposed by the leading Afghan rivals of the Taliban, including the groups favored by the United States.

MG: That was Afghanistan. I will return to the topic of Iraq and other U.S. foreign policy issues later. But first another question, Professor Chomsky: John Lewis Gaddis, whom you consider an important author, has stated that Bush should pursue the same goals in his second term as he did in the first, to insure security in a world that is now more dangerous than ever. Bush's strategies broke with Roosevelt's orientation—he changed course suddenly in response to an attack, and now they are set. One may add that Gaddis considers George Bush and John Adams two of the best strategists among American statesmen. Professor Chomsky, could you comment shortly on these statements?

NC: I am sorry but I cannot be concise. That is a very important book by John Lewis Gaddis, the prominent American historian. He wrote the first book on the roots of Bush's foreign policy, tracing it back to John Quincy Adams, Secretary of State and President. Gaddis is a skilled historian. He cites the right sources, but he does not tell you what they say. In my recent book, *Failed States*, I reexamine them and report what they say. Adams lied to Congress and to the people, and, as the historical record shows, he set a precedent for other presidents to follow: by initiating violent and aggressive wars, by lying to Congress and to the electorate, and by embracing the notion that expansion is the best path to security. Well, today this has come to mean expansion over the entire world. That is what the historical sources say. Gaddis cites them, but he does not convey their content.

MG: The neoconservatives use the medium of speech. In his speeches, George Bush vows to end tyranny, to spread freedom and justice, to strengthen democracy, and to promote dignity and human rights. Professor Chomsky, it seems that you do not believe his promises. Why not? Are these principles not important?

NC: Oh, I think these words are delightful, and you can hear the same promises from every brutal aggressor in history. In fact, it is a worthwhile experiment to look at any despot, even the worst monster, and ask if his words are not noble and uplifting. That is why nobody with any sense pays a moment's attention to the rhetoric that comes from the centers of power. Their speech is devoid of meaning.

MG: A last question regarding U.S. foreign policy before we move on to Iran, Syria, and Iraq. Where should we begin to acquire a new understanding of U.S. foreign policy?

NC: Each case has to be considered on its own terms. There is no universal framework.

MG: But as a general theory, what would be our starting point?

NC: Let us take Iraq. The United States and Britain invaded Iraq, but they have abused the people of Iraq for decades. Both supported Saddam Hussein during his war against Iran, they provided him with the means to develop weapons of mass destruction, they supported him right through his worst atrocities against the Kurds and long after the war with Iran, they supported him again when he crushed the Shiite rebellion that threatened his rule, they imposed brutal sanctions which cost the lives of hundreds of thousands Iraqis, they devastated the society, in all likelihood they prolonged Saddam Hussein's dictatorship, and at last they invaded and turned a disaster into a catastrophe. They have no rights whatsoever. Invading armies have no rights, they have responsibilities. Their responsibility first of all is to pay reparations for the atrocities they have committed, and secondly to comply with the wishes of the victims. We know the wishes of the victims. American and British polls are taken regularly. The latest one revealed that 87 percent of the people of Iraq want a firm timetable for withdrawal; 87 percent means almost all respondents living in Arab Iraq where the troops are actually deployed. So yes, they want a firm timetable for withdrawal. Bush and Blair declared they will not set a firm timetable—they reject the will of the Iraqi people. Of course they refuse to pay reparations. The starting point in Iraq should be that the citizens of the countries themselves and the people of the world compel the politicians to live up to their responsibilities, then we move on from there. Let us take Iran. Iran is now...

MG: We will discuss Iran shortly. Regarding Iraq, there is a theory which argues that what is happening today, while tragic, is only a necessary step in the process of nation building, in accordance with Charles Tilly's phrase, "War made the state, and the state made war."

NC: There is some truth to this. States are imposed and constructed by violence. Just about every state in the world achieved its present borders and its present form by violence and savagery. The state system was imposed on the world by violence. This system evolved in Europe. For centuries, Europe was the most savage and violent place on the planet. Intense internal fighting led to the creation of the state system. Violence and destruction on this massive scale ended in 1945, for a very simple reason: Europeans understood in 1945 that the next time they play the game of mutual slaughter, that will be the end of the world, for they had created a level of violence that threatened to destroy everything. Since 1945, Europe is at peace. But if you look at the centuries that lie behind, they are filled with extreme savagery and violence. And this savagery and violence, which was necessary to impose the state system in Europe, created a culture of violence and the technological means that enabled Europe to conquer the world. Europe has conquered the world, has imposed its state system, each time with violence, savagery, and brutality, the legacy of which persists until today. If we look at the worst conflicts in the world today, they are mostly the residue of the efforts of the European powers to impose state systems which have almost no relationship to the needs and interests of the people concerned. We can run through the conflicts in Africa, South Asia, and the Middle East. Take, say, Iraq. Iraq was created by the British for their own interest, with boundaries that insured that the oil of the north would be in the hands of Britain and not Turkey. The principality of Kuwait was established so that Iraq would have only limited outlet to the sea, and would therefore be dependent. The boundaries were imposed by British power, not by the Iraqis. If we look at the rest of the world, we see the same picture. State systems have been imposed and secured by extreme violence.

MG: Why, in your opinion, does the United States prevent the rise of a democratic and sovereign Iraq?

NC: The United States is opposed to a sovereign democratic Iraq for the same reason that a great power is opposed to sovereign democratic regimes anywhere in the world. The United States has spent most of its history preventing the growth of sovereign and democratic regimes in its own region, in Central America, and wherever it extended its influence. In the case of Iraq, the issue is much more important. Just consider what the policies of a democratic, sovereign regime are likely to be. A democratic, sovereign Iraq would have a Shiite majority, which would try to improve relations with neighboring Iran. They may not love Iran, but they would rather have friendly than hostile relations with it. Furthermore, right across the border in Saudi Arabia there is also a Shiite population, which has been brutally oppressed. Any move towards sovereignty in Iraq would stimulate their efforts to gain minimal rights and some measure of autonomy. The Shiite regions happen to be where most of Saudi oil is. You can imagine that the planners in the Pentagon, Rumsfeld and the rest, are undoubtedly considering their worst nightmare: a loose Shiite alliance—Iran, Shiite Iraq, the Shiite areas of Saudi Arabia—which will control most of the world's oil and be independent of the United States. And it could get worse. They are likely to strengthen their economic and possibly military ties with China, the center of the evolving Asian energy security system, which includes Russia and the states of Central Asia. India is likely to be part of it. If the oil resources of the Middle East are united under one leadership, the United States could become a second-class power. The reasons why the United States is fighting so hard to prevent a sovereign, democratic Iraq are simple and clear—ugly, but clear.

MG: You have mentioned the emerging new powers—China and Russia. Who is benefiting from high oil prices? Will the war on terrorism undergo a metamorphosis, will it take a new direction or change into war for oil?

NC: There have been oil wars for almost a hundred years, certainly since the Second World War. The Middle East is a region of oil wars. In 1953, the United States and Britain overthrew the parliamentary government of Iran because it was attempting to take control of its own oil. Secular nationalism in the Middle East was bitterly opposed by the United States and Britain. They supported extreme fundamentalist regimes instead, because they were concerned that secular nationalist governments, Nasser for example, might try to take over energy resources and use them for internal needs rather than the needs of the great powers. These wars continue to this day. The Iraqi invasion was an effort to intensify U.S. control of the major energy reserves in the Middle East. The same is true in Latin America. Oil wars have been going on since the beginning of the oil age. The difference today is that we have China, and all of Asia, as an emerging power center, or better, a reemerging power center. If we go back to the eighteenth century, China was the industrial center of the world before the imperialist age. And it is recovering its position. China has the fastest growing economy. Its size is now roughly two-thirds of the U.S. economy, and it will draw even in about a decade. It controls most of the world's foreign reserves, and it is not as easily intimidated by the United States as Europe. Right after the Chinese president left the United States, he went to Saudi Arabia, China's leading trading partner in the region. China is also increasing its relations with Iran. And as I mentioned earlier, it is part of an emerging Asian security system, consisting of pipelines, oil installations and so forth, which are part of a global war over energy control. This will undoubtedly shape the future, the near future.

MG: Regarding Iran, Roger Cohen of the *New York Times* wonders which alternative is worse: Iran with nuclear weapons, or a military strike against Iran to block its emergence as a nuclear power. How do you evaluate these alternatives?

NC: Western propaganda presents the problem of Iran as one of Iran developing nuclear weapons. Well, no sane person wants Iran to develop nuclear weapons, and in any case, no one wants anyone to develop nuclear weapons. We do not know whether Iran is planning to develop nuclear weapons, but it is possible. The invasion of Iraq practically instructed Iran to develop nuclear weapons as a deterrent. The invasion sent a clear message: we will attack anyone we like, as long as they are defenseless. To avoid being attacked, you need to develop a deterrent. A solution to the problem of potential nuclear weapons in Iran is crucial, and we know how to proceed. The first step is to withdraw the threats that are instructing Iran to develop nuclear weapons as a deterrent. The second step is to follow the proposal of Mohamed ElBaradei, the head of the International Atomic Energy Agency. Several years ago, he made the sensible proposal that the production of all weapons-usable fissile material—material that can be used for nuclear energy or nuclear weapons—be put under international control. Any country that has a legitimate need for fissile material can then apply to the international agency to obtain it. That would solve a huge problem. If individual states continue to produce fissile material, we are very likely to have a terminal nuclear war. ElBaradei's proposal is very sensible. The United States rejected it, the West rejected it. To date, only a single country has accepted it: Iran. Iran stated that it would accept the proposal, but as far as I know it is the only country. This step would be a move towards an international treaty, which would ban the production of fissile material by individual states. Then there is step three. Two years ago, the European Union and Iran reached a bargain. Iran would temporarily suspend its legal development of nuclear power; in return, the European Union would provide firm commitments and guarantees on security issues, meaning, that the United States would not attack Iran. The European Union backed down from its side of the bargain under U.S. pressure and refused to give such guarantees. That gives us another way to proceed. In May 2003, Iran offered to negotiate all issues with the United States—nuclear weapons, security issues in the region, a whole range of concerns. The United States refused. There are many steps that could be taken to reduce and maybe end the Iranian nuclear crisis, but the United States, Britain, and Europe refuse to take those steps. Therefore, we have a crisis.

MG: Do you side with Francis Fukuyama, who celebrates the victory of liberal democracies, or with Iranian President Mahmoud Ahmadinejad, who wrote in a letter to President Bush: "Liberalism and Western-style democracy have not been able to help realize the ideals of humanity"?

NC: First of all, I do not stand anywhere in that discussion. Both do not mean what they say, so we can dismiss it. Fukuyama and the West are not interested in bringing liberal democracy to the world—we have a long record to demonstrate that. Yes, the words are there, but the words are always there. Let us disregard them and look at the record. It is a record of opposition to liberal democracy, unless it satisfies U.S. strategic and economic interests. I should say that this is recognized by the leading scholars who are also the leading advocates of promoting democracy. I quote: there is "a strong line of continuity" in U.S. policy going back decades and continuing until the present, namely, every president is "schizophrenic." They support democracy if and only if it serves U.S. strategic and economic interests. In other words, the promotion of democracy is mere words, it has nothing to do with actions. We can disregard it, and I also choose to disregard President Ahmadinejad if you don't mind. Where I stand in this is that the peoples of the world should compel their own governments to do what they say. Their words sound all very nice. Let us force them to put their words into action, and let us overthrow those governments who refuse to do so. That has been done throughout history, and it has led to a gradual increase in freedom and rights, never given as a gift by governments, always won by popular struggle. It should continue without end. Yes, the words are very nice, let us praise them, and let us insist that they be turned into actions instead of a situation where the actions consistently conflict with the words.

MG: Regarding Syria, there are different points of view within the U.S. administration. There is talk about changing the attitude of the Syrian government, or the necessity to change the entire regime. In your opinion, what are the real intentions of the U.S. administration towards Syria? And how should Syria respond?

NC: U.S. attitudes towards Syria have followed the general principle: a country is acceptable if it conforms to U.S. goals for the region. For the first President Bush, Syria was fine because it was taking part in his war against Iraq in 1991. When Syria invaded Lebanon in 1976, it was with the support of the United States, because their main task was to kill Palestinians and that was fine. Right now the United States is split with regard to Syria. On the one hand, Syria is criticized a lot. All sorts of terrible things about the regime are said, but those are not the reasons why the United States is critical of Syria; we know that, because the United States is supporting comparable and worse regimes elsewhere. That is not and has never been the reason. The reason is that Syria is the one corner of the Middle East that is not subordinate to U.S. power. It is not accepting U.S. economic programs, the so-called neoliberal programs, it is resisting U.S. orders. Therefore it is unacceptable.

MG: Do you support the Syrian regime?

NC: No, of course not, it is a terrible regime. I am simply saying that the crimes of the Syrian regime are not the reason why the United States is opposing it. The United States supports much worse regimes, and the United States supported Syria in the past when it was serving U.S. interests. The problems of Syria should be handled by the people of Syria, not by a foreign invader who acts out of self-interest and not for the benefit of the population, as history has shown time and time again.

MG: We need to change the attitude of the Syrian regime at a time when it opposes U.S. foreign policy. How can we find the perfect formula to achieve that task?

NC: This way of thinking presupposes that the United States has the right to force governments to conform to its interests, a principle I cannot accept. Russia does not have that right in Chechnya, the United States does not have that right in the Middle East, no power has that right. Yes, there are plenty of problems in Syria. It is a terrible regime in many ways, but those problems should be handled by the Syrian people, and we should help them in that effort in any way we can. Invasions or threats do not help Syria carry out internal reforms. The same goes for Iran. There is a reason why the reformist elements in Iran, which are significant, object to U.S. threats against their country. It makes their government more repressive, more brutal, and increases its popular support. All this undermines the influence of reformist groups. We should support them, support them as people, and enable them to overcome their own internal problems. If Syria, Lebanon, Iraq, the Balkans, or any country in the world moves towards a more democratic and free society, and if that does not happen to conform to the interest of U.S. power—so be it. Let them pursue their own interests. The United States does not have any God-given right to rule the world, any more than Russia had any God-given right to rule Eastern Europe. If the policies of Czechoslovakia in 1968 were contrary to those of the Kremlin, that did not give the Kremlin the right to invade Czechoslovakia. The same principle holds everywhere.

There are serious internal problems in Syria. There was the Syrian occupation of Lebanon. Thus, there are unresolved issues between Lebanon and Syria, and we should assist Lebanon in ridding itself from the remnants of Syrian domination, which, we may recall, was supported by the United States when it was in its interest to do so. Everything should be dealt with internally. In Syria there are many problems to resolve, as there are in Lebanon, as there are in the United States, as there are in any country we look at. They are the responsibility of the people who live in those countries. No outside power has the right to invade a country to solve its problems. Take the terrible problem of the oppression of the black minority in the United States, from slavery to a century of near slavery following abolition (and with a very significant residue that remains; simply look at the hideous prison system, for example)—did any country have the right to invade the United States to settle the problem of slavery (and its aftermath)? It had to be settled internally.

MG: Several U.S. military interventions throughout the world were authorized by international resolutions. What remains of the legitimacy of the United Nations? Does it deserve our trust? Should it remain as it is, or should it be modified? Some figures within the U.S. administration are talking about the need to abolish it.

NC: The relation of the United States to the United Nations is an interesting one. The United States was instrumental in forming the United Nations. In the early years, from the late 1940s to the late 1950s, the United States strongly supported the United Nations—because it controlled it. If we look back at those years, the United States used the United Nations basically as an instrument against its enemies, against Russia and others. That was a residue of the postwar situation, where the United States had overwhelming power. Over the years, the

United Nations changed. As a result of the decolonization in the 1950s and 1960s, the United Nations began to be somewhat more representative of the world's population. Not very much, but somewhat. The hostility of the United States towards the United Nations increased accordingly. There is a good measure for that: the vetoes. The first U.S. vetoes occurred in the mid-1960s. Since the 1960s, the United States is far in the lead in vetoing Security Council Resolutions, Britain is second, and no one else is even close. The United Nations became more representative of a global opinion that is not entirely under the control of the United States and its British junior partner, therefore they veto Security Council Resolutions more often than anyone else. The most serious violation of a Security Council Resolution is to veto it, that is much worse than not abiding by it, and the United States and Britain are far in the lead. There are extremist elements in the United States, for example John Bolton, the U.S. ambassador to the United Nations, who basically says: we have to get rid of the United Nations. What Bolton actually means is that the United Nations is acceptable as long as it follows U.S. orders, otherwise we will disregard it. That is an extremist position, to say that if any force in the world does not obey our orders, we have to get rid of it. I don't have to mention historical precedents here, I am sure you know them anyway. But again, I should say that the people of the United States strongly support the United Nations, very strongly, in fact they want aid and funding to the United Nations to increase. It is surprising, but a majority of the population is even in favor of eliminating the veto and accepting a situation in which the United States will follow the will of the international consensus, even if it runs contrary to U.S. aims. That is a small majority of the population, completely remote from official policy or for that matter intellectual opinion. In fact, it is so remote that the press will not even report the facts.

MG: The media in the United States is influenced by the U.S. administration, and in turn influences public opinion. For example, the media played a major role in convincing U.S. citizens that Iraq was indeed threatening their country. Is it possible to restore objectivity to the biased positions of the U.S. media, and what role do you see for yourself in that process?

NC: First of all, the U.S. media is not very different from the media elsewhere, despite illusions. The United States happens to be a free society, it is the freest society in the world. The government has no power to coerce the media to do anything against its will, which is a very good situation. It took a long time to win that freedom, hundreds of years, but it is there. What the media do is their choice.

The major media happen to be huge corporations, which belong to even bigger corporations. They are closely linked to the main sectors of corporate power, the dominant internal force in the United States, and all that in turn is closely linked to the government. There is a tight, informal linkage between the corporate sector, including the media, and the government. Furthermore, the intellectual community tends to support power, that is a historical tendency everywhere, in the United States as well as in every other country I know. The general effect is that the media more or less transmits the position of state power and corporate power. There are exceptions, pockets of criticism, it is not a hundred percent, but that is the general picture.

In the case of Iraq, in September 2002 the government in essence announced the invasion of Iraq, it was pretty much like that. Condoleezza Rice started giving speeches saying the next thing we will see from Saddam Hussein is a mushroom cloud over New York, he is going to bomb New York with nuclear weapons, he is supporting al-Qaeda, he is responsible for 9/11, and so on. The media picked up the propaganda within one month, and the U.S. population became completely detached from world opinion. People elsewhere might have hated Saddam Hussein, but nobody was afraid of him, they did not think he was going to bomb them tomorrow. In the United States, the majority of the population came to believe that Saddam Hussein is an imminent threat to the United States, and if you look at the polls, that belief correlates very closely to the support of the war, as you might expect. It happens over and over again. Right now, a majority of the population regards Iran as the main threat to the United States. Why is that? Judged objectively, is Iran a threat to the United States? No. It is considered a threat because there is a huge government and media campaign pushing the population towards that belief. These schemes go far back. Maybe it is hard to believe today, but in 1985 President Reagan declared a national emergency because of the security threat to the United States posed by the government of Nicaragua, which is only two days' driving time from Texas. In two days the Nicaraguan army could be invading the United States. I mean it is ludicrous. You don't know whether to laugh or cry, but there was a national emergency, and the population was frightened. That is how governments control their citizens. One of the main methods of control is to inspire fear, and the media play a role in that. They also shape the discussion in such a way that people do not perceive what is happening. A very striking example right now is the Arab-Israeli conflict. The United States and Israel are in effect annexing the valuable parts of the West Bank, and that is presented as "withdrawal." If you read the *New York Times* editorials, they are praising Israel for withdrawing from the West Bank, referring to a policy that annexes parts of the West Bank. That is close to a hundred percent of what has been reported, and consequently that is what people believe.

MG: Professor Chomsky, you are Jewish, and you said you were a Zionist activist when you were young. You are frequently accused of anti-Semitism. How would you defend yourself against that accusation?

NC: Actually, that goes back to the Bible, and I am happy to accept that criticism. King Ahab, who is the epitome of evil in the Bible, condemned the prophet Elijah for being a hater of Israel because he dared to criticize the king's evil acts. All totalitarians throughout history have identified the state with the people and the culture of their country. If you criticize state policy, you are a hater of Israel, of America, of Russia, or any other country you like. I am delighted to be in that company.

MG: When you say that Israeli state practices are similar to Hitler's, is it not justified to call you an anti-Semite?

NC: I have never compared Israel's or anyone else's policies with Hitler's. Hitler was unique. He represents a uniquely hideous development in human affairs. I do not think there was anyone like him. However, I do say that some of the policies mentioned happen to be very similar to his. Hitler's remarks when he took over Czechoslovakia—that is the way great powers speak. We should recognize that. That is not to say that everyone else is committing a Holocaust, of course they are not, that was unique. But we should recognize similarities, planning methods, ways of thinking wherever they exist.

MG: Professor Chomsky, thank you for joining us.

Sabra-Shatila Camp. Poster showing members of the Mikdad family who died in the September 1982 massacre. (photo by Carol Chomsky)

5

Echoes from a Haunted Land

Irene Gendzier

This essay is based on notes written in May 2006. A few weeks later, in July 2006, the refugee camp in Sabra-Shatila, that had turned into an overpopulated and impoverished urban sprawl in preceding decades, made room for hundreds of new refugees from the south. Khiam and Nabatiyeh—both were sites of previous Israeli bombardments—were targeted again in 2006. The Khiam detention center, which had been transformed into a museum and a symbol of Lebanese resistance to the Israeli occupation in the years 1978-2000, was completely destroyed.

This account of the May 2006 visits to Sabra-Shatila, Khiam, and Nabatiyeh occurred under very different circumstances. The legacy of war and destruction, however, was impossible to ignore. So was the glaring poverty that permanently marred the Lebanese south.

May 11, 2006: Reflections on a Visit to Sabra and Shatila

We got out of our cars and walked into the sprawling site of Shatila, late in the morning of May 11. We were scheduled to stay until early afternoon, a four-hour visit to a timeless space—utterly disconnected from the Beirut we had just left—a vast shantytown of impoverished life, dark alleyways, doors without walls, pock-marked reminders of bullet holes crisscrossed by electric wires, uneven floors of open rooms, lines of hanging laundry, and below, a world in motion filled with men, women, and everywhere children running, in apparent disregard of the ruins of their everyday life.

The plan was clear: a day of informal meetings accompanied by our host, Samer, representing Najdeh, the NGO providing vocational training through a variety of programs. We would make a number of informal stops—a meeting with Nohad, mother of three who was herself born in Shatila and now working with Najdeh; a visit to classrooms with the Lebanese intern from Senegal, who came to volunteer as an instructor; a brief visit with the Bulgarian-trained pharmacist; a meeting with trade union and political cadres; and at the end, a visit to the cemetery, the burial ground of the victims of the 1982 massacres.

The visit went as planned, with a generosity and grace that had nothing in common with the rudeness of the environment. But there was another visit—this one unplanned. An invisible journey into a hell of interrupted memories resurrected by the haunted echoes of the forbidden city of the dead, memorialized between a man's coat and a woman's shawl in the Shatila cemetery. There rested those buried in the aftermath of the massacre of 1982, who were everywhere alive and present in the 1982 of 2006.

"Sabra Street and Shatila Camp lie in a popular residential area of Beirut, where there are in fact several small quarters set together. However, because of the presence of Shatila Camp in its midst, the whole district came to be known as the Sabra and Shatila Camps. It was this district's destiny to become the arena of the massacre."[1] In 1982, there were some 20,000 living in the area; the majority were Palestinians and Lebanese, along with Egyptians, Syrians, and Jordanians, among others. The current total figure is an estimated 16,000, of whom half are Palestinians, the others a combination of impoverished Lebanese and Syrians.[2]

On May 11, 2006, we entered Shatila. Noam, Carol, and Assaf followed Samer in one direction to observe a class promoting computer literacy while I went in another, unprepared for what I found. It was the appearance of something that resembled a moving flock of light-footed, laughing pink birds that caught my attention. But they were not birds. The flock was a group of girls between the ages of four and six; the color of starched school uniforms was pink; their laughter was an irrepressible sign of life that stood out as an act of open defiance to the world around them. This too was Shatila, I thought. I asked the instructor, Mohammed, the Lebanese intern who had come from Senegal, for permission to join the group learning to read, write, and draw. Inside, the presence of a stranger evoked giggles and stares, followed by an impulsive exchange of drawings. When I rose to leave, I was taken aback as the young students rushed to the blackboard, filling it with images of trees and flowers, an enchanted forest that was their farewell.

I left with the forest forever embedded in my memory. The flock in pink had given me something unforgettable in their shared and welcoming laughter that continues to inhabit my heart. What would become of them? What future did they have in Shatila, as Palestinian refugees in Lebanon? Would they be able to surmount the obstacles that blocked access to schools, to work, to a future outside of the walls of a camp? How long would Najdeh be able to help them? And what of UNRWA (United Nations Relief and Works Agency) for Palestinian refugees, how long would its resources hold out? The examples set by individuals such as Nohad and Samer were inspiring, but how many would be able to follow?

And what of the legacy that would mark the girls for life? How would they come to learn of it and how would they bear its consequences? I wondered whether they would one day read the account of Sabra and Shatila written by Noam Chomsky, whose relentless struggle to expose the suffering and injustice committed against the Palestinians had brought him to Shatila on May 11, 2006. Would they recognize the experience of their parents and grandparents in Chomsky's *Fateful Triangle*, and that of the others whose fate was intertwined with theirs?

Reading its pages, they would read that "in the first bombing in June [1982] a children's hospital in the Sabra refugee camp was hit, Lebanese television reported, and a cameraman said he saw 'many children' lying dead inside the Bourj al Barajneh camp in Beirut, where 'fires were burning out of control at dozens of apartment buildings' and the Gaza Hospital near the camps was reported hit."[3]

They would learn that Sabra and Shatila as well as the Bourj el Barajneh camp had been "mercilessly bombarded from June 4, when Sabra and Shatila were subjected to a four-hour attack with many casualties...in alleged 'retaliation' for the attempt by an anti-PLO [Palestine Liberation Organization] group with not as much as an office in Lebanon to assassinate Israel's Ambassador to England."[4] And the bombing did not end there.

This was but a prelude to the "Reign of Terror" of September 1982, when some 3,000–3,500 men, women, and children were massacred in Sabra and Shatila.[5] Who would protect them from the cries of the "Palestinian woman who barely escaped being slain Friday night in a refugee camp on the southern outskirts of Beirut [and who] returned to the scene today [September 20, 1982] and screamed for a long time"?[6] This Palestinian woman, in 1982, began screaming when:

> she realized—from the pools of blood in the houses of friends and the bodies that were being uncovered from nearby rubble—that 30 or more of her friends and relatives had been killed.

> She is among the survivors and witnesses who have begun to tell their versions of what happened in the [battered huts and streets of] Sabra and Shatila camps when Israeli-backed Lebanese Christian militiamen moved in on Thursday, a day after the guns of Israeli tanks had pounded the areas. . . . Other witnesses to the events of Thursday and Friday mentioned bright flares in the sky on both nights, and one 18-year-old male patient at Makassad Hospital said the flares came from the Israeli-held stadium just north of the camps. . . .
>
> "Friday evening," he said, "we were sitting in Abu Yasir's shelter." Abu Yasir, he said, was a Lebanese. He estimated there were 50 men, 20 women and about 25 children in the shelter. . . . Armed men entered, he said, and announced that they were Phalangists. The young man later said he did not know there was any difference between Phalangists and Major Haddad's men. . . . The women and children were taken off—to Akka Hospital just south of the camps, the militiamen told everyone. The men were taken out, lined up on both sides of the street and ordered to turn around with their hands up.
>
> He said the militiamen opened fire on their captives, apparently killing most of them. . . . He said that he and a few others were saved by half a dozen Al Fatah guerrillas who suddenly opened fire on the militiamen before they had finished their killing.

Who was responsible for this inferno? The forces of Major Saad Haddad and the Phalangists were under the control of the Israel Defense Forces (IDF).

As Chomsky reviewed the evidence:

> Throughout Thursday night, Israeli flares lighted the camps while the militias went about their work, methodically slaughtering the inhabitants. The massacre continued until Saturday under the observation of the Israeli military a few hundred yards away. Bulldozers were used to scoop up bodies and cart them away or bury them under rubble. One "mass grave that has been specially bulldozed" was directly below an Israeli command center, with a view from an Israeli rooftop position "directly onto the grave and the camp beyond." IDF troops "stationed fewer than 100 yards away, had not responded to the sound of constant gunfire or the sight of truckloads of bodies being taken away from the camps," and told Western journalists that "nothing unusual was going on while mingling with Phalangists resting between missions inside the camps."[7]

Why did no one hear? And what of those who had heard and remained deaf? Would the light-footed flock in pink who had invited me into their enchanted forest some day find sad consolation in the works of a poet who wrote in another time of another place? "No foreign sky protected me, no stranger's wing shielded my face. I stand as witness to the common lot, survivor of that time, that place."[8] Who will stand witness as recorder of this terrible truth?

According to the MacBride Commission, the International Commission on Israel in Lebanon, "Israeli authorities or forces were involved, directly or indirectly in the massacres and other killings that have been reported to have been carried out by Lebanese militiamen in the refugee camps of Sabra and Chatila [Shatila] in the Beirut area between 16 and 18 September."[9]

According to the International Commission: "one of the principal aims of the invasion of Lebanon was to ensure the dispersal of the Palestinian population which was pursued through the destruction of the refugee camps and the massacres at Sabra and Chatila [Shatila]. The terror bombing of civilian areas, especially in Beirut, was partly motivated by a desire to ensure the dispersal of the population. As for the ill treatment of the population, the practice of the forcible assembly of the population on the beaches at Tyre and Sidon resulted in the deprivation of food, water, and medical attention for days, and exposure in the sun. Thousands of persons, especially males between 14 and 60, were systematically detained, many of whom were deported to Israel to be imprisoned. These practices are in serious breach of the Geneva Conventions and Protocol."[10]

The commission's description of Israeli objectives was confirmed by Israeli accounts that claimed that the "first war goal was to destroy the capacity of the Palestinians in Lebanon for any kind of autonomous existence." The second "was based on the premise that it was necessary first of all to bring about a basic change in the internal relation of forces in Lebanon, and then afterwards would come the establishment of a sympathetic regime which was supposed to sign a formal peace treaty with Israel."[11]

There was a third objective, not mentioned in the preceding report. This one rested on Israel's ambitions to control southern Lebanon by relying on its right-wing Christian allies, whom they continued to arm in spite of the massacres at Sabra and Shatila. This arrangement, as described in a December 1982 account, claimed "the 25-mile-deep security zone that Israel wants in southern Lebanon would be off-limits to all artillery, rocket launchers, antiaircraft missiles and fortifications of the Lebanese Army, a senior Israeli official said today."[12] The same zone would also be off-limits to "United Nations or other international military force." Israel had additional demands. It wanted "Lebanon to agree to permit Israeli aerial reconnaissance flights over the area and to allow the establishment of monitoring stations manned by Israelis."

There was, in addition, a fourth objective of a radically different kind. This one sought to destroy memory, not sovereignty or property. According to the *New York Times*, February 6, 1983, "When the Israeli Army invaded West Beirut last September, Israeli troops entered the center [Palestine Research Center], defaced its interior and carried away its entire library, consisting of 25,000 Hebrew, Arabic and English works on the history of Palestinian Arabs and Palestine. It was one of the biggest archives in the world on Palestinian history."[13]

As with the previous goals they failed, while inflicting untold suffering. Their failure was not a matter of mismanagement but of a strategy based on a false political premise. Palestinian autonomy in Lebanon was not destroyed by Israeli policy, but severely curbed. The internal relation of forces in Lebanon was not radically reoriented in Israel's favor. The security zone that aimed to control the south was established. Lebanese allies were found and funded. But the occupation fueled resistance. The result was that the combined resistance of Hezbollah and leftist militants led to the withdrawal of Israeli forces in 2000, and to the strengthening of the very movement that became the object of Israel's invasion in 2006. Then, a different Israeli government redefined its objectives in Lebanon much as its predecessor had done. This time, Hezbollah was the designated enemy as the PLO had been in 1982. The objective of reorienting Lebanese attitudes to undermine support for Hezbollah was to be the prelude to establishing relations with the Lebanese government. But that government rejected such terms while seeking support in the more ambitious struggle in which it was now pitted, one whose impact on the nature of Lebanese state and society has yet to be determined.

Before I left the classroom, Mohammed, the Lebanese intern, turned to me and asked: "Are you an important person?" I explained that I was part of a delegation traveling with Noam Chomsky, Carol Chomsky, and Assaf Kfoury. He asked for no further details, only the chance to express his sense of urgency to Dr. Chomsky, to let him know of the dire need for help, of the harsh conditions of the camp, the ongoing political conflicts, and the desperate need for "help from the top." There was no time to waste, he explained, and not much hope of improvement.

After leaving Mohammed and the classroom, we walked to the pharmacy where the Bulgarian-trained pharmacist, operating in a hollowed-out office, shared with us something of health conditions in the camp and the limited capacity of Shatila's resources, which meant that the seriously ill had to be taken to the hospital at Bourj al Barajneh camp to be treated. The conversation covered the more general constraints facing Palestinian refugees who were unable to find work in Beirut or the means to obtain the requisite accreditation to apply for entrance exams to go to Lebanese universities.

The head of the Palestinian Workers' Union offered a no-less-grim account of the constraints under which he was obliged to operate to protect the interests of his members. Participation in demonstrations with Lebanese unions was hazardous, given the government's view of Palestinians as foreigners. The situation described by the Fatah leader differed in its details, but the conflicts it exposed similarly revealed the political confinement under which Palestinian officials, dependent on Palestinian Authority (PA) funding, operated. Thus, in the light of Israeli policy towards Hamas, funding to the PA was cut—and with it allocations, which had previously been limited as a result of PLO policy, to Palestinian refugees in Lebanon and elsewhere, were terminated.[14] Noam raised the question of alternate sources of funding, as in the case of the Gulf, to which the Fatah official replied that any such funds would, of necessity, first go to those in the Occupied Territories. The possibility of promoting self-sustaining projects, which Noam raised, was not pursued.

How did the people in the camps survive? Nohad and the pharmacist both maintained that there was no malnutrition in the camps. But who had money to purchase the products of Najdeh workshops, or the goods that were sold at outdoor markets run by migrant Syrians? Twenty-four years after the Israeli invasion of 1982 and the massacre at Sabra and Shatila, the camp remained in abject condition.

Shatila is one of twelve Palestinian camps, all of which are marked by the poverty of their inhabitants, that include impoverished Lebanese as well as others seeking safe havens. Of different sizes and in different locations, the refugee camps resemble open prisons, political enclaves with charred memories of their victimization by internal wars and foreign intervention. The list is long, and includes: the 1948 Israeli-Palestinian war, followed by the wars of 1956 and 1967; the 1970 PLO-Jordanian conflict; the 1975 civil war in Lebanon; and Israel's 1978 invasion of southern Lebanon, that was expanded four years later to Beirut and surrounding areas. Then, it includes: in 1985, the "war of the camps" involving Amal and the PLO; and through 1991 and 1992, recurrent Israeli attacks north of the so-called security zone that it claimed since 1978, to include direct hits on Palestinian refugee camps in Ain el Hilwe and Rashidiye. The invasions of 1993 and 1996, in turn, led to the displacement of massive numbers of Lebanese in search of safety. It is of more than passing interest that those years corresponded to the Oslo agreements and the further repression of Palestinians in the Occupied Territories.[15] The situation did not end there for Lebanon, however, as Israel persisted in its attacks and overflights.

With every successive conflict, the number of Palestinians seeking refuge in Lebanon increased, and with the expulsion of the PLO from Beirut in 1982, their vulnerability increased, as did the resolute opposition of the Lebanese state to integrate them. On the contrary, the underlying consensus of the Lebanese political elite was to tolerate Palestinian refugees in the confines of their camps.

As of 2002, UNRWA estimates indicated that there were 402,977 Palestinian refugees in Lebanon, or close to 10 percent of the population.[16] Had it not been for the 1982 invasion and the 1985 "war of the camps" between Palestinians and Amal, it would doubtless have been higher. The presence of Palestinians in Lebanon has long been a source of major internal tension, as the Lebanese state has consistently dealt with Palestinian refugees as foreigners neither to be integrated nor awarded citizenship, but rather to be tolerated until such time as they return home. Repatriation was endorsed by the United Nations General Assembly in 1948, when the first wave of over 100,000 Palestinian refugees fled to Lebanon. It was supported by the United States in the same period. More than fifty years later, it remains among Palestinian demands.

In its October 1949 report to the U.S. president on "United States Policy Toward Israel and the Arab States," the National Security Council stated that "primary responsibility should rest with Israel and the Arab states for solution of the refugee problem"; that, in accord with the December 1948 UNGA resolution, "Israel should accept the principle of maximum possible repatriation of refugees who so desire"; and that Arab states should accept "the principle of substantial resettlement" for those desiring to remain.[17]

For Lebanon's political elites, the integration of Palestinian refugees represents an unacceptable political risk, lest it upset the favorable status quo guaranteed by the retention of the confessional system for those in power. The result is that Palestinians in Lebanon "face some of the most severe protection gaps primarily as a result of political considerations concerning sectarian power sharing in the country along confessional lines. The majority of Palestinian refugees are Sunni Muslims. Integration of the refugee population is regarded as a threat to the sensitive division of power between Maronite Christians, Sunni Muslims, Shia Muslims, as well as Druze, Greek Orthodox, Greek Catholic, Armenian Orthodox, and Armenian Catholic."[18]

For Palestinians living in the camps, the lack of support from the Palestinian Authority, and the continuing opposition to their integration by the Lebanese political establishment, defines the predicament of those who are dependent on the limited resources of external assistance, such as UNRWA (established in 1950), and other NGOs, that are the principal providers of health care, education, and social services.

Assessing the situation of Palestinian refugees in Lebanon in 2003, the International Federation for Human Rights described housing conditions in the camps as "infamously terrible. The extreme overcrowding due to the scarcity of space is aggravated by the prohibition for Palestinian refugees to rebuild the destroyed camps, build new camps or extend the existing ones."[19] Such strict prohibition did not apply to all camps but their overall condition was nonetheless judged as dire.

The situation with respect to employment was no better. A study published in 2004 determined that Palestinian refugees were "barred from employment in nearly seventy different professions due to nationality requirements and the principle of reciprocal treatment applicable to foreigners."[20] Recent legislation appears to have eased some of the restrictions affecting employment, but the qualifications determining access to jobs remain prohibitive. In practice, "entry into professional syndicates and employment is based on the individual having Lebanese nationality for a minimum of 10 years and reciprocal rights for Lebanese citizens in the foreigner's state of citizenship."[21] In short, Palestinians would have to become Lebanese and Israel would have to offer Lebanese reciprocity in terms of employment in Israel. Had such conditions come about, Palestinian refugees would have been enabled to "practice medicine, pharmacy and engineering in Lebanon. . . ."

In October 1982, in a period when Palestinians in Lebanon were fearful of the future, the former prime minister Saeb Salam dismissed the call for the expulsion of Palestinians in Lebanon as impractical. He called, instead, for Palestinians to "stay as long as possible under Lebanese jurisdiction and law," proposing the revival of an official government department to resolve what he termed "the Lebanese question, primarily Palestinians and their diaspora."[22]

The "Lebanese question" today has changed; it is no longer defined exclusively in terms of Palestinian refugees in Lebanon. It is Hezbollah's role and, more generally, that of the Shia community in the Lebanese state system and the future of that system that are critical to the Lebanese question today. The Lebanese question is, from this perspective, an internal matter. But it is one that transcends national boundaries, as the future of Lebanon is inseparable from the broader regional struggle in which the United States and its so-called moderate Arab allies and Israel confront resistance to their hegemony that cannot be reduced to a Syro-Iranian embrace.

The outlook of the Lebanese political elite towards Palestinian refugees in Lebanon has not undergone fundamental change, but the predicament of Palestinian refugees has changed. It has worsened, as they remain hostages of the Lebanese confessional system, all but abandoned dependents of the Palestinian

Authority, and pawns in the outcome of the struggle for a regional order that will influence Lebanon's fate.

Over the years, opposition parties and movements—that were part of the Lebanese National Movement—broke with conservative ranks to support the Palestinian presence. In a recent interview, the secretary general of Hezbollah, Sayyed Hassan Nasrallah, denounced the abysmal living condition of Palestinian refugees in Lebanon, arguing in favor of improved housing, employment, the right to own property, but not the right to citizenship, given existing confessional arrangements in Lebanon. Palestinian refugees should be supported in their commitment to return to their homeland, he maintained. But Nasrallah added that it would be appropriate for other Arab states to share the burden imposed on Lebanon by the Palestinian refugee presence.[23]

The Israeli invasion of 2006 had unanticipated consequences in terms of forging closer bonds between old and new refugees. In the words of Laleh Khalili, the Israeli invasion provided the example of "refugees who give refuge," referring to the Palestinian camps that offered refuge to Lebanese fleeing the Israeli invasion. Thus, camps near Tyre, Saida, and the southern suburbs of Beirut offered protection and assistance.[24] Shatila was host to some "80 of the thousands of families who fled towards the capital" in this period.[25] Hezbollah offered direct assistance to Palestinian camps that had suffered bombardment, while Sayyed Nasrallah personally visited Ain el Hilwe, among the most densely crowded and despairing environments of Lebanon's Palestinian refugee camps.

The long-term impact of such developments is not clear, but for those who sought refuge and for those refugees who provided it, survival was not a function of sect so much as an expression of solidarity among the wretched of the earth.

May 13, 2006: Ten Minutes in the Sun

Sun. Light. Space. They hover as a promise and a threat in this world of perpetual night, where a confined spacelessness overwhelms. Even now, as the doors open and we are invited in to view the museum that has since been destroyed, we grasp something of the meaning of this infamous place whose name has become a synonym for torture: the detention center of Khiam. We follow, one behind the other, under the guidance of Sheikh Nabil Qauq, the head of Hezbollah in south Lebanon, as we look in silence at the sacraments of confinement and torture, reading the names of those memorialized on the walls and in the framed photographic images.

Ten minutes in the sun, but not for everyone. For women, the quotient is ten minutes every ten days. For men, the regime is ten minutes of sun every twenty days. The promise of sun and light comes coupled with access to "an open space," a stark reminder that this claim to power extends to the skies.

The sparse signs that identify the house of horrors that is the Khiam detention center are written in Arabic and English, green letters on a yellow field, the colors of Hezbollah. They convey the pitiless purpose of "solitary confinement," the shameless threat of surveillance, the ominous numbering of "Prison Camp Number 4," the desperate intimacy of "punishment cell 06-05-06," the relentless exhibit of "halls of torture, burying, kicking, beating, applying the electricity, pouring hot water, placing a dog beside," and more. "Until 1988, a prisoner was entitled to one five-minute monthly visit. It was decided then that even that was too much. In early 1995, the visits were reinstated, but only for some prisoners."[26]

Over the years, resistance fighters who belonged to the secular left were the majority of those detained and tortured in Khiam. Included among them was the female prisoner Soha Bishara, tortured by the Israelis for her attempt to kill the head of the South Lebanon Army (SLA); she nevertheless survived her ordeal.

Israel continued to occupy southern Lebanon after 1985, when it withdrew from other parts of the country. A report for Human Rights Watch described the conditions here, disclosing that "captured guerrillas are routinely taken to a prison camp in the village of Khiam in the Israeli-occupied area, where they are tortured at the hands of the SLA, sometimes assisted by officers of Israel's domestic intelligence service (the General Security Service, or Shin Bet)."[27]

Three years later, the United States and Israel signed a "declaration of principles," confirming their cooperation in political, military, economic, and intelligence matters. Khiam was not an unknown; it was simply irrelevant—its larger purpose supported.

Those imprisoned in Khiam were accused of contesting the occupation or resisting those who were its accomplices, and/or being members of organizations, such as Hezbollah, identified with the resistance. The accused, in sum, were charged with opposing either Israeli control over south Lebanon or the control exercised by its proxy army—the South Lebanon Army.

The question of who was in control and therefore responsible for occupation policies, such as torture, was a matter of controversy. An Israeli journalist, Avi Lavie, writing about Khiam put matters simply: "While the South Lebanon Army (SLA) directly manages the installation, it is but a subcontractor, an unskilled worker who takes orders directly from the big boss—the state of Israel."[28]

No students of international law need apply here. In Lavie's words: "In Khiam, there are no judges, trials, lawyers, evidence or arguments. There is no law or judiciary. An Israeli army jeep or SLA Mercedes stops at a house and orders someone to come with them for talk. He might return after one, five or ten years, or perhaps never. Women and children are no exception. At its peak, there were dozens of women in special wards in Khiam. The youngest detainee, as far as is known, was 12-year-old Raba Shahrur, taken for interrogation apparently to put pressure on his brother. He returned home eight months later."

Why Khiam? There is no mystery about the rationale for the operation; no Israeli, Lebanese, nor Palestinian sources indicate confusion as to its objectives. Khiam's morbid identity was an open secret; it was strenuously protected from visits by international relief agencies and journalists. Khiam was a geographical, but not a political, reality. It was effectively erased, except to those—anguished about their fate—within the walls and the residents of the village of Khiam. On May 23, 2000, the citizens rushed the gates and released the living dead.

Khiam was designed to fulfill Israeli objectives in Lebanon. It was part of the "security zone," the Israeli-controlled area justified to the Israeli and Western public as critical to guaranteeing Israeli security against those who objected to the violation of their sovereignty. As Israeli officials conceded, first there were the Palestinian militants; they were beaten. Then there were the Hezbollah militants; they were more difficult to beat. The "international community" does not appear to have been seized with the desire to clarify the legal, moral, military, political, social, or even the human meaning of such policies. This, in spite of the record of pronouncements decrying, denouncing, and ultimately abandoning those incarcerated.

The Lebanese and Palestinians, politely referred to as the "detainees," seem to have played a double role in Israeli policy. They could be held as barely living prisoners to be exchanged for Israeli prisoners, as occurred in the years prior to Israel's forced withdrawal in 2000. But this was part of a more ambitious objective: to control southern Lebanon up to the Litany River. In doing so, Israel would pursue a scorched earth policy that led to the flight and massive displacement of populations, assuming that a change in government "behavior" in Beirut would follow, as a more compliant and assertive regime would prove capable of carrying out Israeli policy as its own.

But as various Israeli political and military figures argued over the years, the "security zone" provided less a guarantee of security than of permanent war. Its advocates claimed to be seeking a strong Lebanese state to enforce the southern frontier, while pursuing policies that undermined the very sovereignty of the same state. For those who were committed to a permanent war with the prospect of eventual occupation of all of Lebanon, the successive invasions

Khiam Prison. Solitary confinement room demolished after Israeli air strike, 2006. (*as-Safir*)

of southern Lebanon demonstrated unquestioned military superiority and political failure.

On May 23, 2000, "perhaps the most-hated symbol of occupation," collapsed as the Israeli-backed South Lebanon Army fled in the face of popular liberation. Five hundred citizens of Khiam descended on the prison, liberating its 144 prisoners.[29]

On May 29, 2006, a delegation from Amnesty International visited Khiam. The detention center of Khiam was turned into a museum, along with its exhibit of an Israeli tank in the courtyard. The Khiam Rehabilitation Center was established.

Then came the next phase of the Israeli-U.S. invasion of Lebanon in July 2006. In its course, Israeli bombing destroyed Khiam's infamous prison. Washington held up pressure on Israel for a ceasefire, allowing no doubt as to its own intentions. Official condolences followed. In September, a report on Lebanon's state of emergency reported on Mine Action undertaken by the UN in southern Lebanon, "13,871 cluster sub-munitions" were among the weapons that had been destroyed. And then there was reference to Khiam in a citation of UN origin:

> According to the UN Office for the Coordination of Humanitarian Affairs (OCHA), 7,000 residents—out of a population of 10,000—have returned to the village of Khiam, Marjayoun District. Initial damage estimates indicate 750 homes destroyed and another 1,000 homes heavily damaged but repairable, as well as an additional 1,000 resi-

> dences lightly damaged. OCHA reports that Khiam is currently without electric power, and the internal water and sewage networks have been destroyed. A generator is providing electrical power to pump water from a natural spring.

For the rest, the past is buried. Its bitter memories are not.

May 13: 2006: The Other Center Holds

We drove from Khiam to another kind of landmark, Nabatiyeh, where the welcome awaiting Noam was only a little short of ecstatic. The program, arranged in advance, included an elaborate Lebanese-style outdoor lunch—simple, elegant, copious, and wondrous—then a break, followed by an informal discussion.

The setting itself was significant, as the Cultural Council of South Lebanon in Nabatiyeh was an historic assembly of prominent left-wing intellectuals of the region. Those who came to participate in the day's events constituted a near permanent flow of supporters who came to hear, engage, and above all, pay homage. No walled-in ceremonies here, the space was open, the mood a friendly chaos in which scholars, teachers, writers, and activists came to listen and express solidarity. The respected longtime activist Habib Sadek, who evoked the memory of the late Edward Said in his remarks on the significance of Noam Chomsky's work and his presence at the Cultural Council of South Lebanon in Nabatiyeh, was lyrical in his welcome and introduction.

We were ushered into the outdoor restaurant, where we were surrounded by smiling faces in a cadre that was oddly familiar. Nabatiyeh, in the early afternoon light, was a painting come to life—a Renoir landscape of festivities in a Lebanese setting. Seated at a table with indulgent neighbors, I had the sensation of being in a kaleidoscope: the green palette of spring vying with the sun's blaze of reds and oranges, pulsating with excitement and a camaraderie that knew nothing of caste or confession.

Yet even in the midst of this celebration, the reminder of other images of war and suffering more akin to Goya's depictions of wars than Renoir's landscapes came to life. Nabatiyeh was in the south, its landscape charred by war, its population decimated by flight. On the afternoon of that sun-swept day of May 13, I accepted an invitation to tour Nabatiyeh with a guest who pointed out various landmarks, including the sign that bore the name of a resistance fighter who had been killed in one of the Israeli advances. Absent from his brother's name was the designation of "*shahid*," the title of martyr that, as he wryly explained, was reserved for Hezbollah fighters.

For those who knew, the mere reference to the Lebanese south evoked not only Khiam, but Ansar, the prison five miles outside of Nabatiyeh, and the historic role of Tyre and Sidon as well as Nabatiyeh, and innumerable other sites in the path of Israeli invasions and the resistance they aroused from the late 1970s through 2000, and again in 2006.

But the Lebanese south has another meaning in Lebanese terminology: it is a synonym for long-term poverty and deprivation, for the politics of neglect by the center. An area rich in feudal history and examples of exploitation by landed families of great power, the Lebanese south was a region of tobacco, its workers, and their resistance. Marginalized by Lebanon's service economy and its politics of indifference, the impoverishment of the south led to a northward migration that contributed to the creation of the so-called belt of misery encircling Beirut. The south, in the interim, became the terrain of opposition parties on the left through the 1970s. It attracted militant, radical, and secular parties such as those organized in the Lebanese National Movement established in 1973 that were committed to abolishing confessionalism, supporting the Palestinian resistance, and promoting socioeconomic development in the south. The left remained active throughout the bitter years of civil war and the period surrounding the Israeli invasion of 1982.

Nabatiyeh was among the cities relentlessly sacked and attacked in that invasion. Its hospitals were targeted. Dr. Chris Giannou and other foreign medical personnel would later testify in the United States about their experiences during this period. Ansar, one of the largest Israeli prisons established after the 1982 invasion, was reported to have held some 11,000 Lebanese and Palestinian prisoners at one point. Israeli military headquarters that doubled as centers of interrogation were set up in other centers, including Tyre, Sidon, and Nabatiyeh, where they generated movements of armed resistance against the Israeli invasion and occupation. It was in this context that Hezbollah emerged. With the parties of the left, it continued the struggle against the Israeli occupation and invasions of the south, including those of 1993 and 1996, that were designed to destroy any forms of resistance to Israel's control over its so-called security zone and those assigned to protect it, such as the South Lebanon Army.

We left Nabatiyeh in the late afternoon of May 13. Two months later, the 2006 Israeli invasion of Lebanon began in the south.

Khiam Prison. Sheikh Nabil Qauq and Noam Chomsky in front of poster of inmates killed under torture. (photo by Carol Chomsky)

6

Meeting Sayyid Hassan Nasrallah: "Encounter with a Fighter"

Assaf Kfoury

The meeting with Sayyid Hassan Nasrallah was organized by Nawwaf Moussawi, head of International Relations of the Hezbollah Party and member of its political bureau. He was also present during this meeting. Preliminary versions of this essay were posted on Counterpunch and ZNet on October 2, 2006.

In the wake of "Operation Grapes of Wrath," the seventeen-day Israeli military assault on southern Lebanon in April 1996, there was a spate of articles in the Western press on Hezbollah and its secretary-general, Sayyid Hassan Nasrallah.[1] The Israeli operation stopped under pressure from the U.S. government, wary of the political repercussions from the mounting toll among Lebanese civilians, including the massacre of more than a hundred refugees in the village of Qana on April 18, 1996. However, humanitarian sympathy for the Lebanese victims did not translate into a less biased image of Hezbollah, typically presented in the Western media as a shadowy and rabidly anti-Western terrorist organization.

There were very few exceptions. In the British press, Robert Fisk in the *Independent* and David Gardner in the *Financial Times* wrote honest and factual articles, including interviews they conducted with Nasrallah in May 1996 and July 1996.[2] The most remarkable article is Eqbal Ahmad's "Encounter with a Fighter," which gives a particularly sensitive and fair account of his meeting with

Nasrallah.[3] Although in English, Ahmad's article appeared in July 1998 in the Egyptian *Ahram Weekly*, at a relatively safe distance from the censorship (and self-censorship) of the mainstream media in the West. But these articles remained all too few and in sharp contrast to the relentless demonization by other journalists and political commentators.

In the U.S. press, more objective views of Hezbollah only occasionally appeared after the year 2000. This was probably elicited by several developments that drew some attention and respect in the West. In the 1990s, in addition to pursuing its guerilla activities against Israeli forces in southern Lebanon, Hezbollah gradually emerged as a powerful political and social movement, promoting dialogue with other Lebanese parties and winning seats for its candidates in the Lebanese parliament. Just as important was the surge in popular support among all Lebanese for the dominant role Hezbollah played in the successful resistance to Israeli occupation, which (mostly) came to an end in May 2000.

In July 2003, Seymour Hersh, an investigative journalist, wrote an article on Syria's situation and the surrounding turmoil—the American occupation of Iraq, the bloody Intifada in the Palestinian territories, and the simmering discontent in Lebanon.[4] Hersh's article included an account of a meeting with Nasrallah, informative and free of the deeply ingrained racism of others. There was also a review in *The New York Review of Books*, by Adam Shatz, the literary editor of *The Nation*, of several books on Hezbollah, for which he interviewed Nasrallah on a trip to Lebanon in October 2003.[5] Although too prone to pass judgment reflecting his own biases, Shatz nonetheless quoted Nasrallah on several issues on which Hezbollah had been persistently misrepresented.[6]

Of all the public statements on Nasrallah, the most startling perhaps, given who the source is, came from Edward Peck. Peck is a former American diplomat and former deputy director of the Reagan White House Task Force on Terrorism, and he was part of an American delegation that met Nasrallah in February 2006. Peck's assessment of Nasrallah was unusually respectful, even sympathetic, and stood in contrast with his earlier impressions of Hamas and Fatah leaders:

> It was interesting to meet with [Nasrallah], because we had already met with leaders of Hamas and Fatah before and after the election was over in Palestine [in January 2006], and his point was a fairly simple one, I think. Talking to us, retired diplomats, Americans, his key concerns were essentially how to free his country from domination…and how to go about building the nation up again, despite all of the things that had happened to it over the years.

> So it was a logical, reasonable presentation. No screaming, no shrieking. You know, just an educated intelligent man talking about serious issues that he perceived. It was interesting in the sense that the projection of people like that in [the United States] is of, you know, blood-soaked wackos, and there are some of those out there on all sides, but that certainly was not the case with him.[7]

We shared Peck's impressions after we met with Nasrallah, a logical and reflective leader, not given to effusive gestures or hyperbole—perhaps at his best when explaining and defending Hezbollah's local politics and role in Lebanon.

On May 11, 2006, we went to meet Nasrallah in a group of four—Noam and Carol Chomsky, Irene Gendzier, and myself—at his heavily guarded compound in the Dahieh, the southern suburb of Beirut, reduced to a heap of rubble by the Israeli air force a few weeks later. Security at the entrance of the building where Nasrallah's office was located, and around it, was extremely high—in sharp contrast with the lacking or half-hearted security measures in the rest of the city.

Nasrallah greeted us warmly, shaking hands with the men, nodding and smiling towards the women. He wore the usual attire of a Shia cleric: turban and tunic. Later, he pointed to the color of his turban (black), which served as a visual sign of someone considered a descendant of the Prophet and the role it enjoins on its wearer in Shia culture, with the smile of someone glad to introduce friendly foreigners to something they may not know.

Our meeting with Nasrallah lasted about two and a half hours. The conversation went from broad generalities at the start, sometimes trite, to specific and nuanced positions on local matters at the end. It started slowly with events in Iraq and Palestine, then covered Iran and regional events, and became more focused as it shifted to the situation in southern Lebanon, and Lebanon in general. We asked a great deal of questions, desiring to hear his perspective.

We did not expect any criticism of Iran from Nasrallah, and we did not hear any. On Iraq, he avoided taking sides in the rift between Shiite factions. He said, "The difference between Ayatollah Sistani and Muqtada al-Sadr is the difference between a wise man in his seventies and an impulsive man in his thirties."

We asked about the prospects for secessionist movements in Khuzestan, Azerbaijan, and other oil-rich areas in Iran. We mentioned that according to some reports, for example, there is an "Ahwazi liberation movement" in Khuzestan. Nasrallah was dismissive of such prospects, maintaining that Ahwazis, as well as other minorities in Iran, are well integrated and well represented in the army and the government.

What of the possibility of a U.S. attack on Iran, or a campaign to force a regime change in Iran? Nasrallah thought it would be a grave miscalculation. "We all see the chaos and destruction created by the American invasion of Iraq, even though it was relatively easy to destroy Saddam's government. It will be far more difficult to bring down Iran's government, let alone invade Iran. Iran's situation is totally different from Iraq's. Saddam's government and army were instruments against the Iraqi people; the Islamic republic in Iran enjoys the support of the Iranian people."

Nasrallah acknowledged Hezbollah's good relations with Iran and Syria, but also insisted on Hezbollah's independence with respect to decisionmaking. We did not press him on the degree of this independence, often questioned by outsiders because of Iran's financial support of Hezbollah. But already in 1996, David Gardner wrote: "Donations from Lebanese Shia in West Africa, from Shiites in the Gulf, and in the form of Islamic tithes have made the organization largely self-sustained." Gardner noted for example that a $100 million complex in the Dahieh with a mosque, hospitals, schools, and research centers was paid for by a wealthy Kuwaiti Shiite, while money from Iran was estimated to be $60 million per year according to Western intelligence sources, but never exceeded $40 million per year according to Hezbollah insiders.[8]

The charge of subservience to Iran persists, chiefly by U.S. government officials still in pursuit of reckless plans to create a "New Middle East."[9] And Hezbollah's leaders keep denying the charge. A few days after our own meeting with Nasrallah, his deputy, Naim Kassem, restated in an interview that his group "has no decision to enter any battle [outside Lebanon] and has said repeatedly that its position is one of defence against aggression." And again: "Hizbollah is not a tool of Iran, it is a Lebanese project that implements the demands of Lebanese."[10]

More to the point, however, longtime observers have dismissed attempts to portray Hezbollah as an Iranian proxy. According to Amal Saad-Ghorayeb, a Beirut-based political scientist who has studied Hezbollah over many years, Hezbollah "has never allowed any foreign power to dictate its military strategy."[11] And according to Ervand Abrahamian, history professor at the City University of New York and a specialist on Iran, "Hizbollah's leaders are not the types to take orders from elsewhere."[12]

An uncertain battle in Iran has for years pitted reformists against conservatives, with the latter now back in power. In our meeting with Nasrallah, this issue did not come up in the drift of the conversation. He referred several times to Iran the country, but did not compare specific individuals or factions in the Iranian government or its opposition. Another issue left aside in our meeting was Nasrallah's views on al-Qaeda and the Taliban. However, in an interview with David Gardner in 1998, he expressed his strong opposition to these movements and presented the Islamic republic in Iran as an alternative model that is sketching out a path for the region towards modernity and democracy. "There are a lot of models. Some of them are very dangerous like the Taliban," he said then.[13] In an interview with David Ignatius in February 2006, Nasrallah categorically set his group apart from al-Qaeda and its actions that are fanning Sunni-Shiite tensions in Iraq. "I believe the most dangerous thing we confront is the so-called Zarqawi phenomenon," he said. "This is a creed of killing without any responsibility—to kill women, children, to attack mosques, churches, schools, restaurants."[14] Nasrallah has often pointed out the contrast with Hezbollah's resistance to Israel, a Shiite organization's action in solidarity with Sunni Hamas and Palestinians. Thus, for example, the prisoner exchange Hezbollah negotiated with Israel in January 2004 involved both Lebanese and Palestinian detainees. And again, when its fighters attacked an Israeli army unit on July 12, 2006, and captured two soldiers, Hezbollah announced it would exchange them for both Lebanese and Palestinian prisoners in Israel.

Turning to Palestinian matters, we inquired about recent events in Gaza and the West Bank, as well as the standoff between Hamas and Israel. Nasrallah said, "The Palestinians' situation is intolerable, we will help inasmuch as we can, and inasmuch as the Palestinians will ask for our help." And then in no uncertain term, Nasrallah said:

> But our own battle stops at the Lebanese border. Whatever the agreement reached by our Palestinian brothers with the Israeli government, it is their responsibility and we will abide by it, even if it is not the agreement that we prefer.

This has been Hezbollah's stated position for years, both to its audience in Lebanon and to the outside world. In 2003 for example, in response to Seymour Hersh, who asked his view on Israeli-Palestinian negotiations at the time, Nasrallah said: "I, like any other person, may consider what is happening to be right or wrong...I may have a different assessment, but at the end of the road no one can go to war on behalf of the Palestinians, even if that one is not in agreement with what the Palestinians agreed on."[15] And again, in his interview with Adam Shatz, when asked whether he was prepared to live with a two-state settlement between Israel and Palestine, Nasrallah said he would not sabotage what is finally a "Palestinian matter."[16]

On the day we met Nasrallah, we spent several hours beforehand in the Sabra-Shatila camp, on the southern outskirts of Beirut. We visited the site of the September 1982 massacre. It was difficult contemplating the dismal conditions of the camp—poor, dusty, and overcrowded—in spite of the warm welcome from everyone we met. The contrast with the glitter and wealth in downtown Beirut was jarring. So, we asked Nasrallah, what about the Palestinians in Lebanon and the camps? He responded: "The Palestinian refugee camps are a disgrace. A Lebanese man will not even allow his dog to live in the miserable conditions of the camps." He continued, "Palestinians in Lebanon should be given the same rights as other Arabs in Lebanon—the right to work, to get social benefits, to own property." As for the option of absorbing the Palestinian refugees into Lebanese society, "Lebanon in its present [confessional] configuration cannot absorb the Palestinian refugees. They cannot be given Lebanese citizenship, and they should be allowed to retain their identity as Palestinians." So, how shall the refugees be helped until the Israeli-Palestinian conflict is resolved? "Other Arab states should help out, Lebanon cannot alone carry the burden of the Palestinian refugees."

We finally turned to internal Lebanese matters. Nasrallah described Hezbollah's political work and the support it enjoys among Lebanese in general. He mentioned, "nearly three-quarters of all Lebanese, both Christians and Muslims, support us and our role in defending Lebanon," and he made a point to stress that this popularity extends beyond the Shia community. (There was a surge of solidarity during the Israeli onslaught of July–August 2006. A poll conducted at the end of July 2006 reported that 87 percent of all Lebanese supported Hezbollah's resistance to Israeli aggression—this is support for Hezbollah's resistance to external aggression, not necessarily for Hezbollah's policies on which Lebanese generally remain divided. A similar survey conducted five months earlier showed only 58 percent of all Lebanese supported Hezbollah's right to keep its arms and, hence, continue its resistance activity.)[17] He explained that the success of Hezbollah as an armed resistance against Israeli occupation was a by-product of its deep roots in the local civilian population. Yitzhak Rabin and other Israeli military men, he claimed, wrote about the difficulty of controlling southern Lebanon as "a land that can be invaded but not occupied."[18]

Though there was no explicit comparison during our conversation between Hezbollah and the Palestine Liberation Organization (PLO) as popular organizations, we couldn't fail noting Nasrallah's comments included an implicit criticism of past attempts to organize armed resistance along the lines of a standing army. In his interview with Robert Fisk in 1996, Nasrallah was explicit; he explained that part of the success of Hezbollah guerillas was that "when they come back from an attack, they will not go to military bases and barracks like the Palestinians did in Lebanon; they will go back to their homes."[19] Pakistani journalist Eqbal Ahmad, who had closely followed the development of the Palestinian movement, also noted the contrast with the PLO, which had projected a pervasive military presence in the 1970s and early 1980s in Lebanon. When he first entered the Hezbollah compound in the Dahieh, Ahmad mentioned his surprise that:

> Unlike the erstwhile PLO compounds and offices in Beirut, there were but few uniformed and armed men visibly around. The stronghold of the most effective armed organization in the Middle East had a completely civilian look, a fact that normally implies intelligent and efficient security arrangements.[20]

The difference was borne out during the war on Lebanon of July-August 2006. In the Israeli invasion of Lebanon in 1982, PLO forces were routed in a few days. In 2006, Hezbollah fighters stood their ground for thirty-four days. In 1982, the Israeli troops reached the Litani River as fast as they could drive their armored vehicles—pushing all the way to Beirut. In 2006, they became bogged down against entrenched guerillas and never reached any point along the Litani River, despite a massive ground offensive of some 30,000 troops in the last two days of the war in which thirty-three soldiers were killed (against a total of 119 soldiers during the whole thirty-four-day war).[21]

We asked Nasrallah, "How do you see the internal situation evolving in Lebanon?" He responded by talking about reforming the electoral system and state institutions so that all Lebanese citizens, both Christians and Muslims, have their fair share in the benefits and services provided by the government. Detractors have accused Nasrallah and others in the Hezbollah leadership of seeking to establish an Islamic republic in Lebanon. These accusations have been unrelenting and typically based on statements and writings from the 1980s, in the early years of Hezbollah, when it openly embraced the goal of an Islamic republic. Since the early 1990s, the Hezbollah leadership has been just as persistent in deflecting these accusations. In his 2003 interview with Adam Shatz, Nasrallah's denial could not be any more categorical:

> We believe the requirement for an Islamic state is to have an overwhelming popular desire, and we're not talking about fifty percent plus one, but a large majority. And this is not available in Lebanon and probably never will be.[22]

Without ever shedding its Islamist character and conservative moral code, Hezbollah has in fact built alliances with other parties, secular and non-Shiite, in order to get a larger representation in the government. When it put up candidates in the last parliamentary elections, some of those on its electoral list were Christians, and it won fourteen seats (out of a total of 128). As noted by Charles Glass, another veteran observer of Middle East affairs, a hallmark of Hezbollah under Nasrallah's leadership has been its ability to change and adapt.[23]

Our last question to Nasrallah was about his party's weapons, an issue that had been debated among Lebanese for many months, and about conditions under which Hezbollah would relinquish its arms. He immediately put the question in a context wider than that of the Israeli-occupied Shebaa Farms, which many of his Lebanese detractors had accused him of playing up in order to justify Hezbollah's retaining its arms. According to Nasrallah, "The bigger issue, the fundamental one, is how to defend our land against Israeli aggression." He mentioned several issues, all reflecting aggressive Israeli policies: near-daily aerial and naval Israeli incursions into Lebanese airspace and territorial waters; the assassination of Palestinian militants in Lebanon; the refusal to release Lebanese detained in Israeli prisons; the refusal to turn in maps of landmine locations in southern Lebanon; and the continued occupation of the Shebaa Farms. And he maintained: "Resolving the problem of any of these issues separately will not resolve the bigger fundamental issue. And it is not a matter of defending only southern Lebanon, it concerns all of Lebanon." He also referred to the need for a "national defense strategy," which:

> We have raised in the National Dialogue conference, and the others agree there is a need for it. Some are asking the Lebanese resistance [i.e., the military wing of Hezbollah] to dissolve itself or be merged with the Lebanese army. But the Lebanese army is small and weak, and given its present organization, from the moment the Lebanese resistance is merged into the army, everything about the resistance will be known by the American government, which means by the Israeli government too—this will put us at the total mercy of Israeli military might.

We asked Nasrallah if we could quote him on things he said during the meeting. He seemed eager to have all of his views transmitted: "Yes, you can quote me on anything, absolutely." As time was running short, we asked him whether he had questions of his own for us. He had one question: "How can we have our point of view heard in the U.S.?" Addressing himself to Noam, Nasrallah asked, "You know better than us the situation in the U.S. If there is anything we can do, any way of explaining our situation so that we can hope for a more equitable U.S. policy, then we need to hear it from you." Noam finished the conversation, stating:

> You need to reach the American public before American politicians. The public in the U.S. is generally ahead of the politicians. Often public opinion conflicts with policies set in Washington. U.S. politicians are usually elected by a minority of the population and represent two parties that are virtually indistinguishable on fundamental issues. If you can inform the public and get them to understand your position, they will put pressure on the politicians and hopefully prevent them from conducting their most destructive policies. Without internal public pressure, U.S. policy is not likely to change significantly.

Beirut, Dahieh. Women walk amid the rubble of destroyed buildings. (AFP)

7

On the U.S.-Israeli Invasion of Lebanon

Noam Chomsky

This essay appeared (in Arabic) in the July-August-September 2006 issue of al-Adab, *a Beirut-based journal of cultural and political affairs. The article was written in response to a request from Samah Idriss,* al-Adab*'s editor-in-chief. The English version was posted on ZNet and several other websites in August and September 2006.*

Though there are many interacting factors, the immediate issue that lies behind the latest U.S.-Israeli invasion of Lebanon remains, I believe, what it was in the four preceding invasions: the Israel-Palestine conflict. In the most important case, the devastating U.S.-backed 1982 Israeli invasion was openly described in Israel as a war for the West Bank, undertaken to put an end to annoying Palestine Liberation Organization (PLO) calls for a diplomatic settlement (with the secondary goal of imposing a client regime in Lebanon). There are numerous other illustrations. Despite the many differences in circumstances, the July 2006 invasion falls generally into the same pattern. Among mainstream American critics of Bush administration policies, the favored version is: "We had always approached [conflict between Israel and its neighbors] in a balanced way, assuming that we could be the catalyst for an agreement," but Bush II regrettably abandoned that neutral stance, causing great problems for the United States (according to Middle East specialist and former diplomat Edward Walker, a leading moderate).[1] The actual record is quite different: For over thirty years, Washington has unilaterally barred a peaceful political settlement, with only slight and brief deviations.

The consistent rejectionism can be traced back to the February 1971 Egyptian offer of a full peace treaty with Israel, in the terms of official U.S. policy, offering nothing for the Palestinians. Israel understood that this peace offer would put an end to any security threat, but the government decided to reject security in favor of expansion, then mostly into northeastern Sinai. Washington supported Israel's stand, adhering to Kissinger's principle of "stalemate": force, not diplomacy. It was only eight years later, after a terrible war and great suffering, that Washington agreed to Egypt's demand for withdrawal from its territory.

Meanwhile, the Palestinian issue had entered the international agenda, and a broad international consensus had crystallized in favor of a two-state settlement on the pre-June 1967 border, perhaps with minor and mutual adjustments. In December 1975, the UN Security Council agreed to consider a resolution proposed by the Arab "confrontation states" with these provisions, also incorporating the basic wording of UN 242. The United States vetoed the resolution. Israel's reaction was to bomb Lebanon, killing over fifty people in Nabatiye, calling the attack "preventive"—presumably to "prevent" the UN session, which Israel boycotted.

The only significant exception to consistent U.S.-Israeli rejectionism was in January 2001, when Israeli and Palestinian negotiators came close to agreement in Taba. But the negotiations were called off by Israeli Prime Minister Barak four days early, ending that promising effort. Unofficial but high-level negotiations continued, leading to the Geneva Accord of December 2002, with similar proposals. It was welcomed by most of the world, but rejected by Israel and dismissed by Washington (and, reflexively, the U.S. media and intellectual classes).

All the while, U.S.-backed Israeli settlement and infrastructure programs have been "creating facts on the ground" in order to undermine potential realization of Palestinian national rights. Throughout the Oslo years, these programs continued steadily, with a sharp peak in 2000: Clinton's final year, and Barak's. The current euphemism for these programs is "disengagement" from Gaza and "convergence" in the West Bank—in Western rhetoric, Ehud Olmert's courageous program of withdrawal from the occupied territories. The reality, as usual, is quite different.

The Gaza "disengagement" was openly announced as a West Bank expansion plan. Having turned Gaza into a disaster area, sane Israeli hawks realized that there was no point leaving a few thousand settlers taking the best land and scarce resources, protected by a large part of the Israel Defense Forces (IDF). It made more sense to send them to the West Bank and Golan Heights, where new settlement programs were announced, while turning Gaza into "the world's largest prison," as Israeli human rights groups accurately call it. West Bank "Convergence" formalizes these programs of annexation, cantonization, and imprisonment. With decisive U.S. support, Israel is annexing valuable lands and the most important resources of the West Bank (primarily water), while carrying out settlement and infrastructure projects that divide the shrinking Palestinian territories into unviable cantons, virtually separated from one another and from whatever pitiful corner of Jerusalem will be left to Palestinians. All are to be imprisoned as Israel takes over the Jordan Valley, and of course any other access to the outside world.

All of these programs are recognized to be illegal, in violation of numerous Security Council resolutions, and according to the unanimous decision of the World Court any part of the "separation wall" that is built to "defend" the settlements is "ipso facto" illegal (U.S. justice Buergenthal, in a separate declaration). Hence, about 80–85 percent of the wall is illegal, as is the entire "convergence" program. But for a self-designated outlaw state and its clients, such facts are minor irrelevancies.

Currently, the United States and Israel demand that Hamas accept the 2002 Arab League Beirut proposal for full normalization of relations with Israel after withdrawal in accord with the international consensus. The proposal has long been accepted by the PLO, and it has also been formally accepted by the "supreme leader" of Iran, Ayatollah Khamenei. Sayyed Hassan Nasrallah has made it clear that Hezbollah would not disrupt such an agreement if it is accepted by Palestinians. Hamas has repeatedly indicated its willingness to negotiate in these terms.

The facts are doctrinally unacceptable, hence mostly suppressed. What we see, instead, is the stern warning to Hamas by the editors of the *New York Times* that their formal agreement to the Beirut peace plan is "an admission ticket to the real world, a necessary rite of passage in the progression from a lawless opposition to a lawful government."[2] Like others, the *New York Times* editors fail to mention that the United States and Israel forcefully reject this proposal, and they are alone in doing so among relevant actors. Furthermore, they reject it not merely in rhetoric, but far more importantly, in deeds. We see at once who constitutes the "lawless opposition," and who speaks for them. But that conclusion cannot be expressed, even entertained, in respectable circles.

The only meaningful support for Palestinians facing national destruction is from Hezbollah. For this reason alone it follows that Hezbollah must be severely weakened or destroyed, just as the PLO had to be evicted from Lebanon in 1982. But Hezbollah is too deeply embedded within Lebanese society to be eradicated, so Lebanon too must be destroyed. An expected benefit for the United States and Israel was to enhance the credibility of threats against Iran by eliminating a Lebanese-based deterrent to a possible attack. But none of this turned out as planned. Much as in Iraq, and elsewhere, the Bush administration's planners have created catastrophes, even for the interests they represent. That is the primary reason for the unprecedented criticism of the administration among the foreign policy elite, even before the invasion of Iraq.

In the background lie more far-reaching and lasting concerns: to ensure what is called "stability" in the reigning ideology. Stability, in simple words, means obedience. Stability is undermined by states that do not strictly follow orders, secular nationalists, Islamists who are not under control (in contrast, the Saudi monarchy, the oldest and most valuable U.S. ally, is fine), etc. Such "destabilizing" forces are particularly dangerous when their programs are attractive to others, in which case they are called "viruses" that must be destroyed. Stability is enhanced by loyal client states. Since 1967, it has been assumed that Israel can play this role, along with other "peripheral" states. Israel has become virtually an offshore U.S. military base and high-tech center, the natural consequence of its rejection of security in favor of expansion in 1971, and repeatedly since. These policies are subject to little internal debate amongst whoever holds state power. The policies extend worldwide, and in the Middle East, their significance is enhanced by one of the leading principles of foreign policy since the Second World War (and for Britain before that): to ensure control over Middle East energy resources, recognized for sixty years to be "a stupendous source of strategic power" and "one of the greatest material prizes in world history."[3]

The standard Western version is that the July 2006 invasion was justified by legitimate outrage over the capture of two Israeli soldiers at the border. The posture is cynical fraud. The United States and Israel, and the West generally, have little objection to the capture of soldiers, or even to the far more severe crime of kidnapping civilians (or, of course, to killing civilians). That had been Israel's practice in Lebanon for many years, and no one ever suggested that Israel should therefore be invaded and largely destroyed. Western cynicism was revealed with even more dramatic clarity as the current upsurge of violence erupted after Palestinian militants captured an Israeli soldier, Gilad Shalit, on June 25. That too elicited huge outrage, and support for Israel's sharp escalation of its murderous assault on Gaza. The scale is reflected in casualties: in

June, thirty-six Palestinian civilians were killed in Gaza; in July, the numbers more than quadrupled to over 170, dozens of them children. The posture of outrage was, again, cynical fraud, as demonstrated dramatically, and conclusively, by the reaction to Israel's kidnapping of two Gaza civilians, the Muamar brothers, on June 24. They disappeared into Israel's prison system, joining the hundreds of others imprisoned without charge—hence kidnapped, as are many of those sentenced on dubious charges. There was some brief and dismissive mention of the kidnapping of the Muamar brothers, but no reaction, because such crimes are considered legitimate when carried out by "our side." The idea that this crime would justify a murderous assault on Israel would have been regarded as a reversion to Nazism.

The distinction is clear, and familiar throughout history: to paraphrase Thucydides: The powerful are entitled to do as they wish, while the weak suffer as they must.

We should not overlook the progress that has been made in undermining the imperial mentality that is so deeply rooted in Western moral and intellectual culture as to be beyond awareness. Nor should we forget the scale of what remains to be achieved, tasks that must be undertaken in solidarity and cooperation by people in the global North and South who hope to see a more decent and civilized world.

Qana. A Lebanese civil defense worker removes the body of a toddler. (Reuters)

8

Beirut War Diary

Hanady Salman

During the 2006 Israeli war against Lebanon, Hanady Salman, the managing editor of the Lebanese newspaper as-Safir, *prepared a diary to document the military aggression, people's stories, and the declining social conditions within the country. She circulated her diary, sometimes more than one entry per day, via email, attaching pictures of people, cities, and buildings ravaged by the Israeli military campaign, hoping to generate international support to stop the war. Hanady writes her diary in the form of an Internet blog (www.worldproutassembly.org/archives/2006/08/from_hanady_in.html). The following is an edited selection of her entries.*

July 16, 2006

You will all have to excuse me for sending this. These are pictures of the bodies of babies killed by the Israelis in south Lebanon. They are all burnt. I need your help. I am almost certain these pictures won't be published in the West, although they are Associated Press pictures. I need your help exposing them if you can. These are people who were asked to leave their village, Marwaheen, this morning, within two hours or else. They were later shot in Teir Hafra. Those who were able to flee went to the closer UN base where they were asked to leave. I think that after the Qana massacres in 1996 when civilians were bombed after they took shelter in UN headquarters, the UN does not want to be responsible for the lives of civilians. A few minutes ago, the Israelis asked the people of Al Bustan village in the south to evacuate their homes. I am afraid massacres will keep happening as long as Israeli actions are unchecked. Please help us if you can.

July 17, 2006

Last night Israel conducted at least sixty raids all over Lebanon, from Tripoli in the north to Baalbek in the east, and in Beirut. Since Thursday, 197 civilians have been killed and 350 injured according to the Health Ministry, but this cannot be completely verified since whole villages and cities are completely cut off; there is no way to reach them or know what's happening there.

Now what happened in the south last night was outrageous. People are fleeing in droves; there are humongous traffic jams in Saida caused by hundreds of people fleeing to Beirut from villages in the south. These people have nowhere to go, which is why they hadn't left their villages before now.

This morning the streets of Beirut were full of families carrying plastic bags in which they had packed their belongings—or what is left of them. Apartment buildings in Beirut are either full or overpriced. Many people have taken relatives and friends into their homes. Now all this is supposed to be fine; it's war: killing, destroying, moving people, cutting off cities, destroying infrastructure. It's classic.

But please—take a minute and look at this picture in a different way. Some countries have said they will help Lebanon's reconstruction. (Thanks.) Saudi Arabia said it will give $50 million in aid. A small calculation of the difference in oil prices between last Wednesday and today will show how "generous" this offer is, especially as the Saudis' political stance was tantamount to giving the Israelis a green light to continue.

Anyway, that was not my point. The point is if you take a real look at the pictures you will see a house, a car, a shop...destroyed. But six days ago these items belonged to real people; they were somebody's car, shop, and house. Inside the houses were toys for children, books, and music. All gone now, and no one will pay for it and it cannot be returned anyway. Only the memories will remain.

The shops are all that these people own. The harbor that was burnt last night contained goods someone paid for. People will go bankrupt. Did I mention that the targeted areas are the poorer ones in Lebanon? The slums of south Beirut, for example. They are teeming with poverty.

July 17, 2006

Today the Israeli government said its "operations" will not end before at least one more week. People are afraid that the next few days will be worse than the past ones. They're expecting that as soon as the evacuation of the foreigners is completed, the Israelis will have a "freer" hand. So people were fleeing madly today. The people who were trying to flee the south and who managed to get out of Saida were trapped and killed when the Rmayleh bridge was bombed from the air. Tyre witnessed more raids and massacres today, and dozens of people are still under the remains of their former houses.

July 18, 2006

Good morning. Last night was another terrible night but there's nothing new about this. The death toll has now reached 220 with 850 injured. One hundred more killed in one day. There was a massacre in a village called Aytaroun in the south. Fourteen people from one family were crushed to death under the ruins of their home. Last night there was an air raid on an army barracks. The Associated Press reports, "'Israeli fighter bombers killed 11 Lebanese soldiers and wounded 35 others in an overnight strike on a Lebanese army base,' the military said on Tuesday, as Israel renewed its attacks on Beirut and northern Lebanon." The problem is the army does not take part in the fighting. Soldiers are being asked to stay in their barracks and wait to get killed it seems. *Ya'ani* (I mean), they could either be asked to go home or to stay and fight. At least then there would be some kind of reason.

July 19, 2006

It's the eighth day. It all started last Wednesday. It seems ages ago.

I didn't sleep last night. Not because of the bombing, although my flat was shaking every time they bombed. They always start their air raids on Beirut around 1:00 a.m. In the other regions they offer 24/7 services.

"Sleepless in Beirut," thinking about tomorrow. Not the next morning, that is, The Tomorrow: houses turned into rubble, burnt bodies, families in the streets, cities and villages under siege, people pleading for food and water…and the Electricité du Liban company sending its people to collect bills!

What would tomorrow look like? What is this happening? They say they want to eradicate terrorism. Why? Would terrorism do more than what they're doing?

On my way to work in the nearby public park I saw Nour, a four-year-old open-heart patient who fled with her parents from the Ouzai area, south of Beirut. Her father wants to stay in an open-door area, he's afraid the "overpopulated" public schools won't be suitable for a child with a heart condition.

"I'm having fun here," she says, smiling to the camera, "we're playing all the time and no one is giving us orders."

Moussa, the guard outside the newspaper building, was crying. His family had just called from their village, Mayss al-Jabal in the south. His wife told him she couldn't find food for their children.

Up to the sixth floor, Bahia, my dear friend and colleague who left her house in Hadath two days ago, was on the phone. Someone was telling her that her house does not exist anymore. She had tears in her eyes when she said, "at least the children are safe."

In my office, the Agence France-Presse news agency confirmed that the four trucks that were bombed yesterday on the Lebanon-Syria highway were carrying food and medicine sent by Turkey and the United Arab Emirates. Reuters reports that in Sel'a, a village in the south bombed overnight, only five of ten bodies buried under the rubble of an apartment building have been found, and they're still looking for the rest. They're all members of one family. Well at least no one will miss them.

Shall I go on? It's still 11:00 a.m. and I have to go see what happened in Ashrafieh, the Christian neighborhood in Beirut, which was just bombed.

July 20, 2006

There are growing concerns that Israel might be using internationally forbidden weapons in its current aggression against Lebanon, although none of this can be confirmed yet. News from the Southern Medical Center, a hospital in Saida (in south Lebanon), is not good.

Dr. Bashir Sham, member of the French Association of Cardiovascular Surgeons, explains that the way the corpses look when they reach the hospital, especially those who died under the air strikes in Doueir and Rmayleih, is very abnormal. One might think they were burnt, but their color is a strange dark color and their bodies look inflated. He says they have a terrible smell. The hair is not burned off and their bodies are not bleeding.

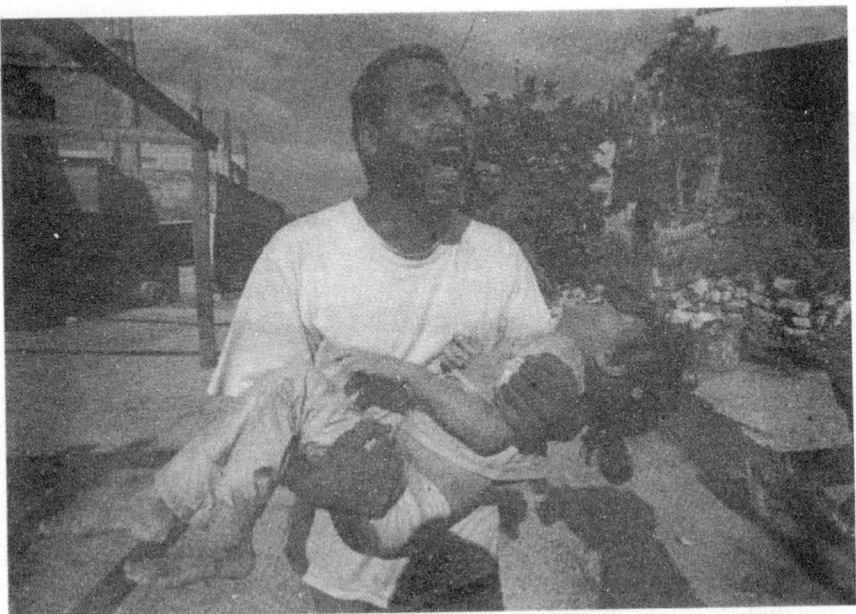

Qana. Man carrying a dead child. (Reuters)

Eight of the victims of an air strike on Rmayleih bridge near Saida on July 15 were transferred to Sham's hospital. Sham says that only poisonous-chemical substances "lead to instant death without bleeding." What indicates the power of these substances is the high and unusual number of dead compared to the number of injuries.

Sham thinks that whatever the "abnormal" substance is that is causing these features might be penetrating the skin. Another explanation could be that the missiles contained a toxic gas that stops the nervous system from functioning properly and causes the blood to clot. These toxic materials cause immediate death, within two to thirty minutes, according to Sham, who admits that these conjectures can't be proven, not even by an autopsy.

The director of the same medical center, Ali Mansour, says the overpowering smell of the corpses prevented him from breathing properly for more than twelve hours after handling them. He explained that the center received eight bodies from Rymeileh last Monday and none of them were bleeding.

Mansour tells us the hospital wrote to both the commissioner of the European Union for Foreign Affairs, Javier Solana, and the United Nations secretary general, Kofi Annan. He said that Dr. Sham will communicate his concerns to the Doctors Order in Lebanon.

July 20, 2006

The fear is growing in Beirut. Beirut is sad, scared, wounded, and abandoned.

By yesterday morning, the UN said 150,000 people (foreigners and Lebanese holders of second nationalities) had already left Lebanon. Evacuations are supposed to be completed by Friday. Today has been an exceptionally calm day. The U.S. marines are evacuating U.S. citizens. By tomorrow the country will be left to its own people and Israel's shelling. By Saturday the only people in Beirut will be those who have nowhere else to go and the very few who deliberately decided to stay. There were also those who managed to flee the south and the southern suburbs of the capital.

What will happen to us on Saturday?

A friend called a few minutes ago scared and begging me to go hide with her in Baabdat in the mountains. She said her friend who works with the UN and lives in Washington called her to tell her to stay out of Beirut because she heard that by Saturday it will be hell. Nothing will stop the Israelis. The city will be theirs. My city, my dearest city, my only home, is open to their warplanes and shells. Our children, as of Saturday, will be the targets of Israeli fire. So it's said.

As of Saturday I fear every city or region will be cut off from the rest of the country. Maybe they won't bomb us. Maybe they will just leave us in our cities and villages to starve and rot to death. Maybe they will do both. Worse than not knowing what will happen is knowing that whatever the Israelis decide to do, nobody will stop them.

July 21, 2006

I have to admit to all of you that I have very mixed, weird, sick feelings about all this. The first three or four days were very strange. I was in Beirut sitting in an air-conditioned office watching the devastation of southern Lebanon and the southern suburbs. It felt like when you watch news and pictures from Palestine and Iraq. You feel frustrated and concerned, but you know there's not much you can do for them, for mere geographical reasons. At least that's the excuse one uses to comfort oneself. But all this was happening a few kilometers away and I was still sitting here watching.

The other weird feeling was related to the first one. I felt that I was paying my dues. The guilty feeling I've always had toward Palestine, and later towards Iraq, has diminished a little bit. I felt like hugging a Palestinian and an Iraqi and screaming to them, "We're with you, like you: left alone, suffering and part of your cause, a great one."

Sometimes I just flip out and cry because I'm so helpless and angry. And most of the time I turn on my "automatic engine." I wake up at six, go to the office, report hideous stories, feel nothing about them, do my job: double check, choose "sensational" headlines, pick out the "best" pictures, try to be as professional as I can be. I do that for twelve to fourteen hours. I then go home, pick up my daughter from my mother's house, and go to bed at one. The Israelis love to start their raids at ten past one, sometimes at five past one. That's when I'm in bed. Every night, when they start, I rush out to the balcony to see where the smoke is coming from. I live on the twelfth floor. Every night, when I go out, I see the moon, my lovely moon, shyly hiding behind the clouds caused by the fires that are surrounding my Beirut.

This morning, I stayed home till noon. I played with Kinda, my two-year-old daughter. My poor little baby. She doesn't understand what's going on. She keeps asking about her cousins. She looks at their pictures and keeps repeating their names as if it were an exercise not to forget them. I tell her they're in the mountains and that we can't go there. When they call us, she refuses to talk to them. She thinks they've abandoned her.

The first time she heard the bombing, she rushed to my arms asking me if this was fireworks. I said, "No, this is boom boom, ha ha ha," and started laughing. So now, every time she hears the bombing she starts singing "boom boom" and she laughs.

When I left, she was sleepy and wouldn't go to bed. It took me a few minutes to understand why. She wanted to fall asleep in my arms. Before July 12, I would not move when it was her bedtime. I'd put her on my lap and sing her to sleep. For ten days now she's been sleeping in the stroller at my mother's house. This is her way of guaranteeing that I will come pick her up when I finish work.

Two last notes: First, I feel ashamed talking about my daughter while other people's children are being killed or unable to get food and shelter. But I feel so guilty that I am not able to spend more time with her. Second, to all the Israelis who have been sending their comments on what I write I say this: I agree with you, we are savages and blood lovers, we don't have feelings and we actually enjoy looking at the pictures of victims. Actually, each time we see one, we party and dance. And in my writings I'm only pretending to have feelings and be pathetically sentimental. It's all a bluff. Here, I'm admitting it. And to all my friends in the West: don't believe anything I say because I'm only viciously using you and trying to turn you into sympathizers of fundamentalist terror.

July 23, 2006

Daily routine: I wake up to the sound of a close one (shell). The radio is on all night long. So is the TV. I listen to and look at what I missed in my sleep. Last night they bombed Saida where my aunt and her family live; they bombed Akkar in the north, they bombed the southern suburbs of Beirut, they bombed a factory in the western Bekaa and they bombed, for the first time in its history, my village—Chmestar, in the eastern Bekaa.

I get up, fix breakfast for my own personal refugees and start my daily phone marathon. (Don't tell the Israelis the landlines are still working.) I start with Saida; my aunt pretends to be strong. She tells me the bombing was far from their house. When I spoke to her son he told me a mall, very close to their house, was hit.

I call my friend in the north: all is fine. My other friend in the western Bekaa tells me the Israelis brought a factory down, a big one it seems that used to build prefabricated houses and hangars and export them to Iraq. But that wasn't all: some miracle happened early this morning when the shelling spared Al Hanane Institution, where tens of orphans live: the whole area was bombed like hell.

I need to mention that Hezbollah does not exist in the north or in west Bekaa. These are Sunni areas (that do not like Hezbollah anyway).

I call the family house in my village. They tell me there are over forty people living in the house because we have a basement. It seems that Israeli fighters flew over the village all day yesterday, took pictures, and then bombed at dawn. They bombed the graveyard, where my grandfather, my uncle, and my cousin are buried. My cousin tells me that my ailing grandmother is not well, she's ninety and she's sick, and it seems that for three days now she has been unable to recognize anyone or anything. If she dies now, we won't even be able to take part in the funeral. There are no passable roads. But if she dies now maybe it will be less heartbreaking because everyone else is dying: young people, children (the estimates say 170 children were killed by Saturday, July 22).

Then I call my sister who found refuge in the mountains. All are fine. The last phone call was to my sister-in-law, my brother's wife who fled to Syria (her mom is Syrian). They're staying in Bloudan, a town closer to the Lebanese border than Damascus. She told me they could hear the bombing on Baalbek and the rest of the Bekaa all night long.

Hanady the weirdo: Here are some more of my sick thoughts. I need to tell you that ever since this started, I've been keeping myself busy 24/7 because I don't want to have time to think about anything. But sometimes I can't help it. You know, when I'm taking a shower or trying to fall asleep. I get these weird thoughts. I try to get rid of them but they keep coming back. Sick thoughts.

Yesterday, I thought I was completely mad because I found out that somewhere deep down inside of me I fear the moment when all this will be over. What would happen then?

Nabatiyeh. Highway entering Nabatiyeh town destroyed. (*as-Safir*)

We'll be left with the dead, the injured, the ruins, the refugees, the diseases, the misery of those who lost everything, all this destruction, no roads, no phones, no electricity (you know how long it takes to repair this sector?), no water, and a corrupt, impotent government.

We'll be left without the attention we are getting now. Crimes have to be really bad to be able to draw the world's attention. Look at how indifferent we all are towards each other during times of conflict and suffering. It took something as horrendous as the massacres in Rwanda to shake us awake for a while. Who remembers Africa now?

Back to earth. The thing is that all this destruction happened so fast. (Congratulations to all the scientists working on "improving" arms and their effectiveness. They're really doing a great job that nobody seems to appreciate.) I can't believe, for instance, that when this is all over, if we're all still alive, I won't be able to reach my own village. Everything is so fast and it is all reported live. It makes it somehow unreal—as if you were watching a movie. I just can't seem to be able to grasp the idea that this is actually happening. What do you call this? Denial?

Extracts from the story of my life: There's something else that explains my sick feelings and thoughts: my history. I'm thirty-eight years old. I was seven when I witnessed my first war. I was fourteen during the 1982 Israeli invasion of Lebanon. Seeing all this wreckage, all these villages completely wiped out, the fires, the injured, the dead, all of it takes me way back in time and I stick to the idea that these images are not of what's happening now; instead, they're pictures of old houses that were never rebuilt after the last war was over. That's what I tell myself. I need to, because I fear that the moment I realize that this is actually happening here and now I'd explode…literally.

I can't believe the kind of articles we were working on in the newspaper just twelve days ago. I still have the minutes of the last meeting: two people covering a mini-campaign to change the family laws that grant children to their fathers after divorce; two other people following the lobbying efforts for granting women the right to give Lebanese nationality to their children if they're married to foreigners.

July 24, 2006

She's much prettier than her pictures, Huwaida. Despite what they did to her. The one safe eye she still has is green, sad, and beautiful. The stitches that go all the way down from her right eye to underneath her neck, are almost as deep as the look in her eye.

She was sitting on her bed, very silent, very small, so small. Her aunt was trying to get her to eat. Jelly, custard, cheese, chocolate, fresh orange juice. There was everything on that tray. Everything any child would want.

Only when she saw the books my colleagues brought her, did she have something that looked like a twinkle in her eye. The one eye they left her.

She's Fatma's roommate. Lucky Fatma, she has her mom and her sister next to her. They were injured too; they stay in the room next door. The whole family is at the same hospital, although on different floors. Huwaida's parents are not there.

Huwaida's father, her sister Abla, and her brother Ahmad were in the garden of their small house in Marjayoun in the south when the Israelis went hunting. Huwaida was in the house with her mom and other sister. So they didn't die.

I don't know who brought Huwaida to Beirut. It was probably her aunt who's staying with her. The mother and sister were taken to another hospital. Nobody dares to tell Huwaida what happened. She speaks to her mom on the phone. She keeps asking for her brother, Ahmad. Her Ahmad has left her, but she doesn't know it yet.

She holds her tiny sandwich with her banded hand. She bluffs, she's not eating, she's somewhere else, that look in her eye, the only thing they left her, is so deep, it's not the look of a seven-year-old. It's that of a much older person. A wise one. Experienced. Someone who's been through things other people don't even know exist.

It's the same look in Fatma's eyes. Fatma turned twelve today. We got her a cake with some candles that we weren't allowed to light so as not to hurt her lungs. Her whole body was burnt. She and her family were in the car fleeing Bleeda to Tyre in the south; they believed the Israelis who'd told them to evacuate the village before it was too late. They should have known better. They should have known they were going to get them anyway, anywhere.

Wise—not only the looks in their eyes were wise. Wise was the way they both handled us, with our stupid cake, our presents, our fake smiles; smart us, acting as if nothing has happened, is happening. Sad, no other word in the world can describe it more. Sad. So sad it makes your heart ache, and your faith shiver.

July 25, 2006

Today, the UN "peace-keeping" forces evacuated a number of civilians from some villages in the south. Only those who hold Western nationality were evacuated. The holders of Lebanese passports were begging the UN to take them along. *They did not*. They just left them there to die.

Do they tell you about this in your newspapers? Do they tell you that the UN "humanitarian" envoy who came and toured *my* country was lecturing the refugees with that patriarchal, arrogant know-it-all/seen-it-all, trying to look sweet-and-compassionate-with-other-species look in his eyes?

Do they tell you that this same guy, whose monthly wage is probably higher than the yearly revenues of all those who died today, concluded that *my* country needs $150 million in humanitarian aid, and that once he reached Cyprus, he concluded all this was Hezbollah's fault?

Do they tell you we're not beggars? Do they tell you we don't need charity? Do they tell you we work for a living? That we earn whatever we have? That we sweat, we sing, we read, we learn, we breathe, we love, and we hate.

That woman, Huwaida's aunt, is not a beggar. She's all alone with her burnt niece in a Beirut hospital. Four days ago she had a house and a family. Four days ago she had a life. Yesterday, when I gave her the hundred dollars Rola had given me for the people in need, she cried so hard it made me want to die.

Dignity. That's what it's all about.

July 27, 2006

Yesterday was not a particularly good day. I was completely devastated, and had a lot to do. First I had to take care of Um Mustafa, a seventy-five-year-old

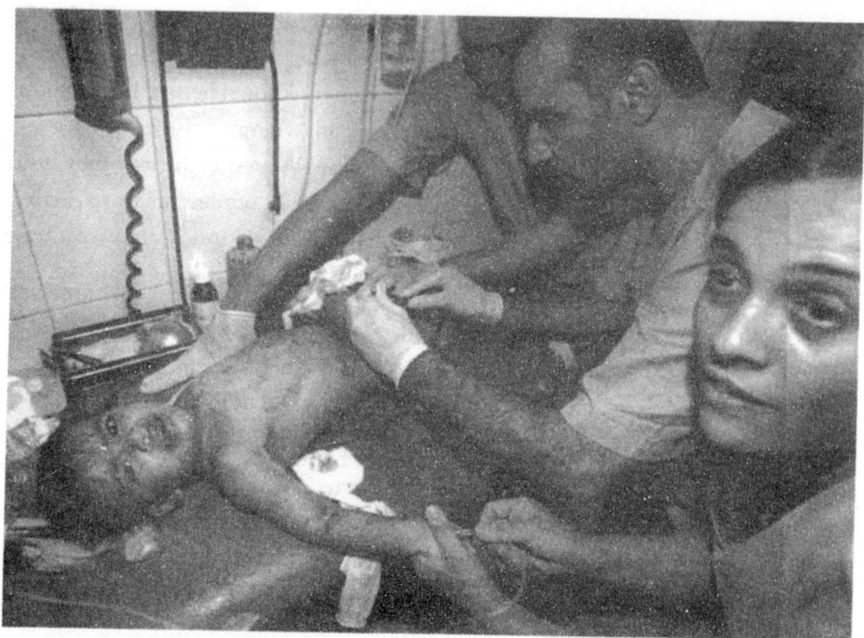

Beirut, Chiah. Emergency room after an Israeli air strike. (AP)

Egyptian lady who has been cleaning houses in Lebanon since the 1970s. My friend Leila said we'd better get her out of here, she doesn't have to go through all this. She's not feeling well, she's getting poorer every day because no one wants to hire an old lady, who can barely move, to clean their houses. I don't think you want me to describe to you the room (Is it a room? It's something with a roof on the top of it.) where she lives.

So I called my friend Yasser at the embassy and he was very helpful. However, we discovered that the lady was wanted by the Lebanese authorities, and that if the embassy takes her to the border she will be arrested. For two days we tried to find out what crime she committed; what is it she did that gives her only two choices in life: stay here and get killed by Israeli air strikes or go to jail at seventy-five. After an in-depth investigation, we found out that she hadn't renewed her work permit or other papers since 2000. She'd have to pay $1,200 (U.S. dollars) or rot here for the rest of her life.

Thanks to the embassy's efforts, we got her out. Most Egyptian workers here do not have permits. If the embassy hadn't done something about it, I think the Lebanese authorities would have seized the opportunity to collect some money.

So, Um Mustafa is now in Syria, (I hope) on her way home.

July 27, 2006

Sad stories in the paper today. A colleague went to see a family in Zahra Hospital in Beirut. They told her how they fled Tireh village in the south: their house was bombed, some family members were buried under the rubble and the rest went to the neighbors' house. But it was also hit, and under its ruins were left more family members. The rest had to flee. Their car was targeted on the road. More of them got killed. They met a UN convoy and screamed for help. One UN soldier took their picture but when he finished he yelled, "No, no," and he left them there. Now the father and two sisters are in a hospital in the south and the rest of the family is in Beirut.

My other colleague toured some of the schools hosting refugees with a group of doctors. Disease is spreading rapidly. When you don't have water or washing machines; when tens, sometimes hundreds, of people share school rooms, this is bound to happen. She also met a group of some thirty people who could not find a place in one of the public schools and who are now in the garden of an empty house. She tells the story of the eighty-year-old woman there who wouldn't eat because she wanted to spare the food for the children. The woman told Saada, my colleague, it would be a waste for her to eat when the children are hungry.

The minister of health announced today that 600 people were killed and some 1,300 injured since Israel began its onslaught on July 12. George W. Bush says he's against a ceasefire that does not solve the problem from the roots. Well, tell him it's working: we're being murdered from the roots.

August 1, 2006

Three of my colleagues went to Tyre today. I will spare you the details of what they saw and wrote. There is only one thing that I need to share with you. Saada went to Jabal Amal Hospital. There she found the following: a four-year-old boy, Hassan Chalhoub, had spent the previous night between the dead in the morgue. A day before, he had been sleeping next to his sister Zeinab, six, in the shelter in Qana. His mother was there, too, and his father, who is in a wheelchair. Many of the people of Qana are survivors of the 1996 massacre when 106 people were killed and more than 100 injured in Israeli raids on civilians who had sought shelter at the nearby UN base. Many of the people of Qana have special needs, if you understand what I mean.

Hassan was sleeping when it all happened Saturday night. His mom was injured but she managed to find her way under the rubble and was looking for her children. She called to him and he answered her. She asked him if he was injured and he said no. She went to look for her daughter and husband. She found her daughter's hand. She tried to pull her up. She couldn't. Then she saw her husband so she crawled to him. But before that she caressed her daughter's hand and whispered to her, "Forgive me my angel for being unable to help you out of here."

She saved her husband, believing someone had already taken care of Hassan. She and her husband spent the rest of the night in the house where the civil defense workers had taken them. The next morning, they were taken to the hospital. Hassan was thought dead. He was put with the other dead children. He woke up in the morning and opened his eyes only to see a two-year-old girl lying next to him. He thought she was sleeping. He looked around and luckily found a man. He asked, "*Ammo*, what am I doing here?" The man couldn't believe his eyes.

He took Hassan to his parents. When Hassan saw his mom he started yelling at her, "Why did you leave me there alone, sleeping with our neighbor's children? How could you? You know, if I weren't scared I would have followed you home. But it was dark and they were shelling, so I slept again. Where is Zeinab?"

His mother told him the following: "She's having fun in heaven. There are no Israelis there, she's happy there."

August 1, 2006

We just learned that the mother of our senior reporter, Hussein Ayoub, was killed in her village (Aynata) in the south. She had been missing for five days. She was staying with the rest of her neighbors at a house they figured was safe in the village. Five days ago she left them and said she was going to stay with her sister who lived one block away. Hussein managed to call his aunt two days later and she told him his mom never came to her house.

Today, the Red Cross confirmed they have found her body along with two other people in the woods near Aynata. They were trying to flee the village on foot. Hussein's father was killed by the Israelis too, in 1978.

August 2, 2006

Hussein's mother's story hit us all very hard here at the newspaper. We went to see Hussein to pay our respects but were told that his mother may not be dead; they can't find her body. It's the same for so many other victims and their rela-

Qana. Casualties of the Qana bombardment. (AP)

tives. Because so many bodies are still under the rubble in their villages and since most of the victims in the hospitals are disfigured, dismembered, and therefore unidentifiable, nobody knows who's dead and who's still alive.

Actually we still don't know where Hussein's mom is. The last thing we were told was that she was not among the bodies that were brought to Tyre, but the Red Cross told us there were still four bodies in the center of Aynata that couldn't be recovered under the shelling. Hussein went to Tyre today where there is heavy shelling in the city and on the roads to and from it. We're all holding our breath. Yesterday, the pictures of the people of Aytaroun leaving their hometown—children, elderly, poor men and women, all trying to run for their lives, same as the people of Bint Jbeil the day before—seemed more than any human being could bear.

August 4, 2006

Good morning. We're still alive, despite last night. They were busy bombing Gaza, South Lebanon and Baalbek, until 3:14 a.m.; that was when they started hitting the outskirts of Beirut. There were twelve or thirteen air strikes? I stopped counting at the twelfth strike and fell asleep. Don't ask me how, I don't know.

My husband and "my refugees" were out on the balcony trying to locate the new targets, but I stayed in bed. I had a terrible migraine and couldn't even open my eyes. I'd open them only with every new explosion, and listen to the correspondent on the TV specifying the number and targets of each. They were all falling on Ouzai, south of Beirut.

This morning we discovered they'd hit fisherman's spots; two or three associations for orphans and people with special needs; and a place where the Rabab Sadr Charity Association keeps donations (clothes, medicine, etc.). I don't know how many people got hurt yet; our reporter is still there.

This morning, Israel bombed four bridges north of Beirut, killing five and injuring fifteen. (This figure is not final because some are still under the rubble.) The bombings closed the one remaining road out of this hell to Syria. The international press headlines this morning are, of course, "Nasrallah threatens to bomb Tel Aviv." Perhaps one can excuse these presses: they went to print before 3:14 a.m. Only I don't understand why CNN and BBC still cling to that headline. Nasrallah said, "If you bomb Beirut, we'll bomb Tel Aviv." That was it. So, what the Israelis are doing is bombing the outskirts of Beirut. (Smart, right?)

Reports say that the coming three days will be very harsh. (Harsher?)

In any case, for the last three days we've been busy with a very complicated matter: among the one million refugees, there are many people with special needs. There is one main reason for that: most of them are from the south and were injured in previous wars or were victims of landmines; and then there are those who were born with special needs.

These people are going through hell in the public schools. These schools are not equipped for the disabled, autistic, or epileptic children whose conditions are getting worse with all these people crowded around them. The refugees are mostly rural, fairly educated people, but clearly incapable of handling these "special" situations on top of everything else. Whenever one of our special friends has a crisis, the other children get scared, some even complain, and the parents of the "special" refugees try to keep their children "hidden." One mother with an autistic child has been living in a bathroom with her kid, refusing to get out, refusing to let the people from the Disabled Association see her kid. She lives in complete denial, refusing to admit that there's anything wrong with her child, and she's scared to death they might take him away from her.

August 6, 2006

I had nightmares last night. Lots of them. I woke up I don't know how many times to find out I was only dreaming. Denial is a big issue over here. You see, if we were to grasp the whole scope of what's happening, we'd spare the Israelis a whole lot of U.S. taxpayers' money. We'd all die from natural causes, such as heart failures and the like.

OK, I will give some reasons why I dread the day when this war will be over. First, we already have *one million* refugees all over this (tiny) country. What can any state, country, or government do with one million refugees? November is almost two months away, that's when the winter season settles in for real. Second, think of the wiped-out villages. Who's going to remove all the rubble? No one wants to think now about rebuilding. It took us some fifteen years and some $40 billion in debts to do it once before, and the debts have yet to be repaid and the rebuilding is yet to be finished.

Third, there are scattered families who still have hope that once this is over they might find their loved ones. What will happen when they find out how many of them died? If all these people start crying together, at the same moment, hard enough, I mean as hard as anyone would cry when they lose one family member, and then there will be others crying even harder because they will have lost more than one family member. How far away will they be heard?

A fourth reason are the strange diseases starting to spread because of the physical presence of so many corpses outdoors everywhere in the south and elsewhere. By the time this bloody war is over, these diseases will have killed many more.

Therefore, the one thing I'm hoping for right now is a twenty-four-hour truce so we can bury the dead and empty the hospital morgues. Then, they can start over, and go on as much as they like, pushing as far as possible toward the day when our wall of denial will have to fall.

August 10, 2006

Hell started early today.

It seems it will be hell all over Lebanon. Israel bombed Beirut half an hour ago. They bombed an old lighthouse, so old no one even remembers when it was built. It's some seven buildings away from my house. But it is also some four buildings away from Hariri's house.

There was a small army unit based under that lighthouse which had aerial transmissions that belong to the Lebanese Public Radio (LPR). They hit another transmission aerial, in Amsheet, to the north of Beirut. It was on top of an old building that LPR has not used in years. There was a small army unit based there too. They're bombing Baalbek in the east, Beddawi in the north, and they're hitting every single village from Tyre to Naqoura in the south. Most hospitals have no further fuel reserves. There is a ship loaded with fuel that came all the way from Algeria and has been waiting in the poisoned Lebanese waters for days for an Israeli "OK" to come in. The two generators we have are out of order and they're cutting the electricity in some fifteen minutes. So, I'm writing this in a hurry.

August 10, 2006

In the al-Bass Palestinian refugee camp in Tyre, Shi'a villagers from the south took refuge. They say the Palestinians are going out of their way to make them feel at home. They let them borrow money and sometimes use their own savings to buy food for the refugees. The Palestinians say this is the least they can do for those who have been hosting them on their land for fifty years. It takes a refugee to know what it means to be one.

August 15, 2006

This will probably be my last letter to you. I will miss you all. Some of you I have never met, but I feel that you are all so close to me. More than that, you probably already know: without you I would not have made it through this hell. You were there by my side and that made me stronger. Every day, you gave more meaning to all this. People's stories were heard, people's suffering was shared. This was what I could do for my people: tell some of their stories. Knowing that you would listen, knowing that you cared, made the whole difference.

As of yesterday new stories are coming in: those returning to find...nothing. Those returning to find their loved ones under the rubble. But returning anyway. 7:00 a.m. was the official time for the ceasefire on Monday morning. People were on the roads at 7:00 a.m. sharp. I am so proud. Sad, hurt, but proud. Proud of my people, proud of their resistance, proud of their commitment and dignity.

Hussein Ayoub, my colleague, finally found his mother today. Ten minutes ago actually. He went to Aynata in the morning and the rescuers were able to pull her out of the rubble of a house where she, and some seventeen other people, had taken refuge. We don't know when she was killed. But at least he was able to recognize her body. She was seventy-five.

We will be fine, I hope. We will bury our dead, the way they deserve to be buried; we will remember them as long as we live. We will tell their stories to our children; they will tell their own children the story—the story of a great people, one who never lost faith despite all the crimes, pain, and injustice. One that started rebuilding the minute the fighting stopped—rebuilding although they know that the enemy might destroy everything again, as it did so many times before.

We will also tell them the stories of our enemy: how they killed our children and our elderly; how they hit us from the air, from the sea, and from the ground; and how we prevailed. We will tell them: how they starved our families in their villages, killed them on the roads, and bombed their houses, their shelters, and their hospitals. They even bombed the vans carrying bread to them—but we never gave up.

My grandmother used to tell me how people starved during the First World War. I used to think I would never have similar stories to tell Kinda. Kinda, my heroine, Kinda my sweet little heroine who now, every time she hears the sound of a plane, rushes to my arms, points to the sky, and says: "Israel, *Huwaida wawa*!"

Kinda, my baby who survived her first Israeli aggression. For that I will always be grateful, and I promise I will never forget that other babies were not spared. For them I will keep telling Kinda the story. For them, Kinda will never leave this land. Kinda will know who her enemy is. Kinda will know this enemy cannot beat us. Kinda will grow to respect all the men who fought for her on the front lines, and those who will rebuild her country again. Kinda will also grow to know how important all of you were in her life that painful summer in 2006.

Aitaroun. Lebanese refugees from the town of Aitaroun in southern Lebanon. (AP)

9

Dispatches from Beirut

Rasha Salti

On July 11, 2006, I landed at Beirut airport late at night. I had been living in New York City for eight years, and I planned to relocate back to my home in Lebanon that summer. July 12, 2006, was supposed to be the first morning of the new chapter in my life. Instead it was the beginning of a nightmare.

As soon as I heard the news flash that Hezbollah had captured two Israeli soldiers, I called some journalist friends. All believed that Israel would strike back with force, but I refused to accept this. I sent an email to friends I had just bid farewell to in New York claiming Israel's retaliation would probably be swift and limited, that they ought not to worry. The next day, with bitter reluctance, I came to accept the reality that Israel intended to unleash a brutal military campaign. The two kidnapped soldiers were to provide nothing more than the pretext. I then drafted a second email acknowledging with dread what was about to become another devastating and destructive war against Lebanon.

A number of those who received that email asked for permission to forward it to others and I agreed. It was dispatched under the subject heading "From my friend Rasha in Beirut." The next email I drafted was also forwarded. I began to receive requests from people—some I knew, others I did not—to be included on the list of recipients. During the first week of the war, I wrote every day; quickly, however, it became impossible to do this. Written at first in the tone of private conversation with friends, my own commentaries ultimately proved insufficient. I felt compelled to transform other people's stories into testimonials of the injustice and suffering that people were then facing every day. By the third week of the war, the act of bearing witness became itself insufficient to stave off the overpowering sense of anger and helplessness. I joined a group of people to launch a campaign of "civilian resistance." We started planning for an action to break the Israeli siege of south Lebanon with a convoy of cars that would go to targeted and ravaged towns and deliver food and medicines. Planning for the action was so time consuming that I stopped writing. The last dispatch was sent a week before the date set for the convoy to depart. What follows are the dispatches I wrote until that point in the war, signed "Rasha from Beirut."

—Rasha Salti

July 14, 2006

I am writing now from a café, in west Beirut's Hamra district. It is filled with people who are trying to escape the pull of twenty-four-hour news reporting. Like me. The electricity has been cut off for a while now, and the city has been surviving on generators. The old system that was so familiar at the time of the war, where generators were allowed a lull to rest, is back. The café is dark, hot, and humid. Espresso machines and blenders are silenced. Conversations, rumors, and frustrations waft through the room. I am better off here than at home following the news live; on-the-spot documentation of our plight in sound bytes.

The sound of Israeli warplanes overwhelms the air on occasion. They drop leaflets to conduct a "psychological" war. Yesterday, their sensitivity training urged them to advise inhabitants of the southern suburbs to flee because the night promised to be "hot." Today, the leaflets warn that they plan to bomb all other bridges and tunnels in Beirut. People are flocking to supermarkets to stock up on food.

This morning, I wrote in my emails to people inquiring about my well-being that I was safe, and that the targets seem to be strictly Hezbollah sites and their constituencies. Now, I regret typing that. They will escalate.

Until a few hours ago, they had only bombed the runways of the airport, as if to "limit" the damage. A few hours ago, four shells were dropped on the buildings of our brand-new, shining airport.

The night was harrowing. The southern suburbs and the airport were bombed from air and sea. The apartment where I am living has a magnificent view of the bay of Beirut. I could see the Israeli warships firing at their leisure.

July 14, 2006

It is now nighttime in Beirut. The day was heavy, busy with shelling from the air and sea, but so far the night has been quiet in Beirut. We are advised to brace ourselves for a bad night, although at this stage, analysis is like reading tea leaves.

In the present conflict, a secular, egalitarian democrat such as me has no real place for representation or maneuver. Neither have I nor my ilk succeeded in carving a space for ourselves, nor have the prevailing forces (the two poles) agreed to make allocations for us. That is our defeat and our failure. In Lebanon, we are caught in the stampede and the crossfire. I am not a supporter of Hezbollah, but this has become a war with Israel. In the war with Israel, there is no force in the world that will have me stand side by side with the Israeli army or the Israeli state.

The "showcase" last night began with Israeli shells targeting Hezbollah leader Hassan Nasrallah's home in the southern suburbs. As soon as the shells exploded, the media reported them and waited to confirm that he and his family had survived. About half an hour later, the newscaster announced that Hassan Nasrallah planned to address the nation and the Arab world by phone.

I never thought he was charismatic, but a huge majority of people do. He's very young to hold the position of leadership that he does. He's a straight talker, not particularly eloquent, but speaks in an idiom that appeals to his immediate constituency in Lebanon but is also compelling to a constituency in the Arab world that harbors disillusionment, despondency, and powerlessness with the failed promises of Arab nationalism to defeat Israel and restore dignity. He is not corrupt; he lives simply, and displays a bent for spartan asceticism.

He began by declaring an open war on Israel's assault. He reiterated that Hezbollah did not fear an open war; that they have long been prepared for this confrontation. Interestingly, he claimed that they possessed missiles that could reach Haifa, and "far beyond Haifa, beyond, beyond Haifa," thereby admitting that it was Hezbollah that fired the missiles to Haifa (until then Hezbollah denied having fired them). It is not clear what he meant by "far beyond Haifa." Did he mean Tel Aviv?

July 15, 2006

Today was a bad day. The shelling started in the morning and has not let up until now. Tonight the shelling is again focused on the southern suburbs, Haret Hreyk and Bir el-Abed. The first neighborhood is where the headquarters of Hezbollah are located. They have been targeted several times and there is extensive damage.

The leadership has not been harmed. A great number of the inhabitants have been evacuated, but the afternoon shelling targeted residential areas. I am up, anxious, writing—as if it served a purpose.

Foreign diplomatic missions are making plans to evacuate their nationals. They had planned to evacuate people by sea, but after today's shelling of the ports, they may have to rethink their strategy. Should I evacuate? Does one turn their back on a "historic" station in the Arab-Israeli conflict? I was shamed this morning for having these thoughts. And now, at 1:30 a.m., as the Israeli airplanes fill up my sky, I am writing them again.

July 16, 2006

Things seem to be heating up. Missiles hit Haifa and the shelling on the south and southern suburbs of Beirut is unrelenting.

Israeli prime minister Ehud Olmert promised scorched earth in south Lebanon after missiles hit Haifa. Warnings have been sent to inhabitants of the south to evacuate their villages, because the Israeli response to Hezbollah will be "scorched earth." As major roads are destroyed and the south has been remapped into enclaves, it is not clear how these people are supposed to evacuate—or to where. So Hezbollah dragged us, without asking our opinion, into this hell. We are in this hell, caught in this crossfire together. We need to survive and save as many lives as possible. The Israelis are now betting on the implosion of Lebanon. It will not happen. There is *unanimity* that Israel's response is entirely *unjustified.* We will show the Arab leadership that it is possible to have internal dissent and national unity, pluralism, divergence of opinion and face this new sinister chapter of the Arab-Israeli conflict.

July 17, 2006

We live now from "breaking news" to "breaking news." I have been in the café for one hour now. This is what I have heard so far:

- A text message traveled to my friend's cell phone: A breaking news item from the Israeli military command: "If Hezbollah does not stop shelling Galilee and northern towns, Israel will hit the entire electricity network of Lebanon."

- Hezbollah shells Haifa, Safad, and colonies in south Golan.
- A text message traveled to my other friend's cell phone, from an expat who left for Damascus and is catching a flight back to London. "All flights out of Damascus are cancelled. Do you know anything?"
- Israeli shells fell near the house of the bartender. His family is stranded in the middle of rubble in Hadath. He leaps out of the café and frantically calls to secure passage for them to the mountains.
- Hezbollah downed an F-16 Israeli plane into Kfarshima (near Hadath). There is slight jubilation in a café that thrives on denial.

"Breaking news" becomes the clock that marks the passage of time. You find yourself engaging in the strangest activities: you catch a piece of breaking news, you leap to another room to announce it to family although they've heard it too, and then you text message it to others. At some point in the lineup, you become the "messenger" of breaking news. Along the way you collect and send other pieces of breaking news. Between the two sets of breaking news, you gather up facts and try to add them up to fit a scenario. Then you recall previously mapped scenarios. Then you realize none of them worked. Then you exhale. And zap—until the next breaking news comes, it just gets uglier. You fear nighttime. For some reason, you believe the shelling will get worse at night; when vision is impaired, when darkness envelops everything. But it's not true. Shelling is as intense during the day as it is at night.

There has been "intense" diplomatic activity between yesterday and today. UN envoys, ambassadors, EU (European Union) envoys, all kinds of men and women coming and going carrying messages to the Lebanese government from the "international community" and the "Israeli counterpart." Officially, they have led to nothing.

I started writing these dispatches to friends outside Lebanon to remain sane and give them my news. I was candid and transparent with all my emotions. The ones I had and the ones I did not have. By the third dispatch, I was getting replies, applause, and rebuke from people I did not know who had read them.

A journalist from Israel's Channel 2 emailed me and asked for an interview. I was uncomfortable with the idea at first, fearing that my words would be distorted and my genuine, candid sentiments quoted to serve arguments I do not endorse. The journalist seemed like a nice person, but I have no reason to trust her, and she understands my misgivings. She sent the set of questions below for me to answer so she can air them on TV or use them for some report. I decided to share them with you all (her statements and questions are in italics):

1. How does your day look from the morning? What did you do today? Did you have coffee? How do you get the news—television? Radio? Internet?

The routine of our days is totally changed. We now live under a regimen of survival under siege. Those of us still not wounded and not stranded do whatever needs to be done to survive until the next day. Coffee, yes, I have coffee in the morning, and at noon, and in the afternoon. Perhaps I have too much coffee. The passage of time is all about monitoring news, checking to make sure everyone's OK, and figuring out what has to be done to help those in distress. News is on all the time.

I am at home now, listening to the radio on one side, writing emails on the other side. Air-conditioning is on. I live in the center of the city. Later I will go to the office. I think life in my city continues but at a lower volume.

Life as it was, or as previously understood, in my city has stopped. No gym classes, and I am accumulating cellulite, hence chances of finding second husband are lessened. (Can I make the Israeli army pay for that?) Air-conditioning is dependent on electricity or the generator working. Power cuts are the rule now and the generator works only on a schedule. So yes, without air-conditioning and with power cuts, my "Semitic" curls produce an unruly coiffure and I have to admit, I am enduring the siege with bad hair.

2. Can you describe the neighborhood you live in?

So it will be bombed? No thank you. I live in a very privileged neighborhood, far from the southern suburbs. After the evacuation of foreign nationals (and binationals) is complete, everyone is expecting doom, and if the Israelis decide to give us a dose of tough love as they did in the southern suburbs, my life will probably be in serious danger as will my family's and everyone who has decided to stay here.

3. Can you say something about yourself—like what you do for living?

I organize cultural events and I am a freelance writer. I used to live in New York City and moved to Beirut on Tuesday, July 11, 2006. I have no life at the present moment. I try to do a few things over the Internet, but that's increasingly difficult.

4. In Israel, our leaders think that targeting Hezbollah and other places in Lebanon will turn the rest of the local population against them. Is this true?

It is pure folly, but even if it were true it is a terrible strategy, an imploded Lebanon is a nightmare to all, not only the Lebanese, but to everyone. Does Israel want an Iraq at its doorstep? There seems to be consensus now in Israel over the military campaign. It is because Israelis are not yet asking their leadership and military the smart questions. Do you actually believe it would be possible to eliminate the Shi'i sect from Lebanon, and that it would go down easy in the region? If the Americans are advising you, duck for cover or move. Need I list their record of wisdom and foresight recently? Vietnam, Central America, Somalia, Afghanistan, Iraq. If you need to listen to imperialists, find less idiotic ones, at least those who have a sense of history. God help us all if Rumsfeld is also in charge of your well-being. This war will bring doom to all. Stop; cut everybody's losses. Wars can be stopped before the body count is "intolerable" or an entire country has been reduced to rubble.

5. What is the atmosphere in the streets of Beirut?
Beirut is quiet, dormant, huddled. We are caged, but there is tenacious solidarity. You have to understand that we see ourselves under an unwarranted attack from Israel. The capture of two soldiers *does not* justify Israel's response.

6. What is the atmosphere among your friends?
The consensus is solidarity. Our country is under attack. Otherwise, we are an exceedingly pluralist society: everyone has a theory and a point of view, and we coexist, humoring one another.

I hope you will wake up to the nightmare you have dragged us into, will want a ceasefire as soon as possible, will deem our humanity as valuable as your own.

July 18, 2006, 11:30 p.m.

I have about half an hour before the generator shuts down. Most of Beirut is in the dark. I dare not imagine what the country is like.

Today was a particularly strange day for me because I was granted an opportunity to leave tomorrow morning by car to Syria, then to Jordan, and from there by plane to wherever I am supposed to be right now. For days I have been itching to leave because I want to pursue my professional commitments, meet deadlines, and continue with my life. For days I have been battling ambivalence towards this war, estranged from the passions it has roused around me and from engagement in a cause. And yet when the phone call came informing me that I had to be ready at 7:00 a.m. the next morning, I asked for a moment to think. I was torn. The landscape of the human and physical, the depth of destruction, the toll of nearly 250 deaths, more than 800 injured, and 400,000 displaced binds me to a sense of duty. It was not even patriotism; it was actually the will to defy Israel. They cannot do this and drive me away. They will not drive me away.

I decided to stay. I don't know when I will have another opportunity to leave.

July 22, 2006

One of my closest friends, my beloved sister really, Maria, left two days ago. Up until a few hours before she was supposed to follow instructions from the British embassy for evacuation, she could not get herself to leave. She has two boys, aged nine and five. Maria and her husband lived in London for a long while and earned citizenship there. Everyone who matters in her life called and urged her to evacuate with the Britons. She had moved from Beirut to the mountains on the second day of the siege. Our phone conversations had the rare virtue of being "constitutional," they charged our respective systems and reminded us of the people we once were, the lives we once lived. We asked the same questions over and over: "Should I leave?"; "Should you leave?" She did not want to, but felt she ought to for the boys.

She caved in two days ago. I called as she waited on the docks with her two sons. Her husband did not want to leave. "It's awful, it's awful," she kept saying. "It's awful, it's awful," I echoed her. She pleaded, "Have I done the right thing?" I replied, "Absolutely," without a hint of hesitation. I could not help telling her that I would miss her. It felt selfish, needy in the way children can be self-centered and dependent. In truth I was terrified of living through this siege without her. I felt like a good part of my heart, at least a good part of what I love about being in Beirut, was standing at the docks waiting with her two sons.

July 23, 2006

I accompanied journalists to Haret Hreyk two days ago. I suspect I am still shell-shocked from the sight of the destruction. I have never, ever seen destruction in that fashion. Western journalists kept talking about a "post-apocalyptic" landscape. The American journalists were reminded of Ground Zero. There are no gaping holes in the ground, just an entire neighborhood flattened into rubble. Mounds and mounds of smoldering rubble. Blocks of concrete, metal rods, mixed with furnishings, and the stuff that made up the lives of residents: photographs, clothes, dishes, CD-ROMs, computer monitors, knives and forks, books, notebooks, tapes, alarm clocks. The contents of hundreds of families stacked amidst smoking rubble. A couple of buildings had been hit earlier that morning and were still smoking; buildings were still collapsing slowly.

I was frightened to death. I stopped in front of one of the buildings that housed clinics and offices that provided social services. There seemed to be a sea of CD-ROMs and DVDs all over. I picked up one, expecting to find something that had to do with the Hezbollah propaganda machine (and it is pretty awesome). The first one read "*Sahh el-Nom 1*," the second, "*Sahh el-Nom 17*." *Sahh el-Nom* was a very popular sitcom produced by Syrian TV in the 1960s.

Haret Hreyk is also where Hezbollah had a number of its offices. Al-Manar TV station is located on the block that has come to be known as the "security compound" (or "security square"), the office of their research and policy studies center, and other institutions attached to the party. It is said that in that heavily inhabited square of blocks more than thirty-five buildings were destroyed entirely.

One of the buildings was still burning. It had been shelled at dawn earlier that day. Clouds of smoke were exhaling from amidst the ravages. The rubble was very warm; as I stepped on concrete and metal, my feet felt the heat.

July 26, 2006

My dispatches are beginning to disperse. I write disjointed paragraphs. I cannot discipline myself to write every day. I miss the world. I miss life. I miss myself. People around me also go through these ups and downs, but I find them generally to be more resilient, more steadfast, and more courageous than me. I am consumed by other people's despair. It's not very smart—I mean for a strategy of survival.

I am haunted by the nameless and faceless caught under rubble, in the undergrounds of destroyed buildings or simply in the midst of its ravages, waiting to be given a proper burial.

July 26, 2006—later that day

I have tried to the best of my ability to keep up to date with professional commitments from my former life. It's almost impossible, but if I stop I know I will fall apart entirely. It is surreal to write emails following up with work. The world outside is decidedly distant. The mental image of my apartment in New York City is practically impossible to summon. Avenue A, the deli at the corner, and the Yemenis who own it, all lapsed. This is what happens when you are under siege. My friend Christine said to me yesterday that she forces herself to go to the office to keep from going insane, but she cannot remember anything about her work before the siege started. The sound of Israeli air raids comes every so often just low enough to spread chills of horror and fright. But the droves of displaced who arrive here every day have transformed the space of the city. Their wretchedness is the poignant marker of the war.

I spent the afternoon yesterday in Karm el-Zeytoon, a neighborhood in Ashrafieh (a Christian area of east Beirut, that translates literally as "olive grove") where some schools have been opened to house some of the displaced from the south and from Beirut's southern suburbs. I played cards with a six-year-old child who had one elbow in a cast and eyes sparkling with humor. An elderly, overweight woman came over and asked R. to find her and her sister a room. She could not tolerate the heat or the mosquitoes in her old age and health condition. She begged her. She wanted to die in dignity, not like that, on a mattress in a school. She could barely hold back her tears.

I left them reluctantly.

July 28, 2006

Throughout the war, shelling, siege, grief, and sorrow, the bougainvilleas have been in full, glorious bloom. Their colors are dizzying in their intensity: purplish red, boastful fuchsia, glaring white and sometimes canary yellow. Most of the time, their bloom, which is the objective outcome of "natural" factors, namely, access to water, sun, heat, and even perhaps wind, has irritated me. Everything has changed in this time of war, except the full glorious bloom of the bougainvilleas. Other flowering trees have wilted, or shied, as their franchised gardeners or patrons no longer operate on the same schedule or have evacuated on the ships of the binationals.

On the road to Saida, I was struck, irked, and even upset at the bougainvilleas' full bloom. Between their abundant leaves and flowers, vignettes of the ravages appeared: bridges torn in their midst framed by the purple and fuchsia bloom of the bougainvilleas.

We drove along the old road. It had not survived unscathed. There were small holes in its middle, and pieces of rocks, cement, and debris. From within the winding inner roads, the new highway was visible and the big craters from the shelling.

The coastal road would have been bustling at this time in the summer with expats, binationals, students on summer vacation, and tourists. This is the stretch of the south's most visited beaches. They range from the very fancy to the modest. At this time in the summer, the roads would have been busy with the town's handsome beach boys, tanned, strutting in swim trunks and a claim to some local fame. Everything was eerily deserted. Even army soldiers, posted in spots with seemingly no rhyme or reason, walked cautiously, expecting to duck for cover at any moment. Life all around had folded and packed.

We drove by closed homes, doors locked, windows shut, shutters sealed. The last gaze of their dwellers still lingering on the front porches, the gaze of a hesitant farewell that quickly ran a checklist to make sure all was safely tucked away and hoped for the best, maybe even whispered a prayer or invoked God or Christ's clemency and then hurried into the car and sped away for a temporary safer haven.

The bay of Saida appeared and the coastal highway leading to its seaside corniche was entirely deserted. The bridge that unloads traffic from the highway onto the corniche had been pounded. Carcasses of cars lined its sides, some buried under blocks of concrete. We drove around and turned and entered Saida from roads tucked behind. The orange groves were dizzyingly fragrant. Car traffic inside the city was heavy. Pedestrian traffic was heavy.

Saida had received more than 100,000 displaced until two days ago.

I was told people were renting entrances of buildings to sleep at night, or the garages of cars. So far more than eighty-five schools were housing all these displaced, in addition to an old prison and the building of the court of justice.

The building stood on a hill overlooking old Saida and the fort. There was a soft gentle breeze and all was quieter up on that hill.

We were guided by one of the administrators. The floor was inundated with natural light. Even the corridor was well lit. The rooms were spacious, and fit with four beds. The floor was not at full capacity.

In the next room lay two elderly women. A son sat next to one of the women and was caring for her. The other elderly woman had physical disabilities and could not walk. She was from Abbassiyeh. She had been left behind. The mayor of that village had dropped her off and left. She did not speak. No one knew anything about her. She carried no identity papers. She lay in bed and stared into the garden. Her gaze was not unfocused. In fact, it was intent. I have rarely seen such sharp, pure, and focused sorrow. We moved around her room and she did not budge. The hospital administrator greeted her, to no reply.

We drove back the same way. My heart had never felt as heavy. There was a lot to hang on to. I looked forward to the fragrance of orange blossoms and was now forgiving to the full glorious bloom of the bougainvilleas.

Ghaziyeh. Mourning the dead. (AP)

10

Gaza War Diary

Mona el-Farra and Laila el-Haddad

Mona and Laila happen to be related: aunt and niece, respectively. Mona el-Farra is a medical doctor by training and a co-founder of al-Awda Hospital, located in the Jabalia refugee camp in the Gaza Strip. Laila el-Haddad is a journalist who travels frequently. She divides her time between the United States, where her husband Yassine works, and Gaza, where her parents live. (Yassine's own parents survived the August 1976 Tel Zaatar massacre outside Beirut, having escaped a few weeks earlier to the Wavel refugee camp near Baalbeck in the Bekaa valley where Yassine was born.) Both Mona and Laila write diaries in the form of Internet blogs: Mona's "From Gaza with Love" (http://fromgaza.blogspot.com/) has been online since March 2006, and Laila's "Raising Yousuf" (http://a-mother-from-gaza.blogspot. com/) since November 2004. In their diaries, they often refer to each other and to members of their extended families, in Gaza and Lebanon.

Prior to the thirty-four-day war in Lebanon, from July 12 to August 14, and for six months since Hamas won a majority of seats in the Palestinian legislative elections in January 2006, Gaza had been subjected to a systematic campaign of political and economic strangulation, culminating in the Israeli armed assault on Gaza on June 28. The following is a selection of entries, edited in consultation with Mona and Laila, from their diaries during June, July, and August 2006. Entries by Mona are in plain characters, and entries by Laila are in italics.

June 9, 2006: Gaza—On the Beach

Afternoon, 4 p.m., Hoda age twelve, with her brothers and sisters, is running happily, giggling, racing to reach the beach, while her dad and mom are busy carrying the picnic basket. It is Friday, and like other Palestinians, Hoda's family is trying to enjoy a little fun. It serves as a moment's escape from the hardship of daily life—economic sanctions from Israel, the European Union, the United States, military siege, four months with no salaries for more than 160,000 government employees, a Palestinian economy already vulnerable and impoverished, the high unemployment rate, an unsettled political situation, factional clashes, weak health services, lack of vital medications, widespread psychological problems, and children suffering from malnutrition. The moment shattered. An Israeli gunship suddenly fired at random against the beach, while army tanks fired artillery shells and Apache helicopters crossed the sky. Ten civilians killed, forty injured.

I watched Hoda on the local TV—shocked, yelling, crying, "*Ya baba, ya baba*" ["O dad, o dad"]. Her father's dead body was on the sandy hill unable to answer the child's plea; her mother was killed along with Hoda's three brothers and sisters.

Hoda arrived at al-Awda hospital with dozens of injured and dead. The child was in a state of denial. She kept saying to me, "Mom and dad did not pass away, they are at another hospital!" Whole families were destroyed in minutes. And all I heard was: "The Israeli army will investigate the incident." U.S. officials commented on the right of Israel to defend itself! I personally have no comment. Like many of us in Gaza, I burst into tears. Some of my colleagues at the hospital could not go into the child's room. The cameraman collapsed at the scene.

Friends...last week while I was at al-Awda hospital, I visited the health emergency crew, who were targeted while evacuating the dead bodies of resistance fighters, after a battle between the Israeli army and the resistance movement. One of the injured was Dia Halaby, age twenty-seven, a member of the hospital's health emergency team. Ten civilians were injured, as well as a local radio news reporter. The ambulance was heavily damaged, though it was clear it was a rescue team. I tried to report what I heard from Dia and others, but I couldn't write. I felt this was one of the normal practices of the Israeli army, to attack health emergency teams. I wonder, is it our destiny as people living under occupation, to deal with abnormal practices as if they were ordinary normal events? Friends, please help me to stay strong, so I can continue helping others.

June 9, 2006: Bloody Friday— Ten Killed in Gaza Massacre, as Shelling, Sonic Booms Continue

Just as I've made my way back to Maryland, getting ready to post about how the rest of my trip went, and for my stint on* Democracy Now *with Amy Goodman this

morning, I learned that ten Palestinians were killed by Israeli shelling in northern Gaza as they were picnicking on the beach. Three of them were children, two under the age of two. And their mother. Forty others were wounded. We called my aunt Mona, who works with al-Awda hospital in Gaza. She was hysterical, and this is a woman who seldom loses her grip.

She just spoke of blood and body parts, and how one of the cameramen at the hospital couldn't hold it together and dropped his camera as he was filming after he heard a bloodied, battered girl crying out for her father.

After a week of energizing talks, in which I felt I could contribute a little bit by informing people, I feel so useless being here, so impotent and angered, I just want to cry and scream.

My aunt said the dreaded sonic booms had resumed and Israeli warplanes were shelling the Khan Yunis area. And just last night, I was talking about how the sonic booms, under pressure from human rights organizations, had seemed to cease. I spoke too soon.

The horror continues, and the main headline on Yahoo's sidebar is: "Hamas to resume attacks in Israel." I guess that answers Amy Goodman's question to me this morning, "How do you think all this is being conveyed in the media?"

June 13, 2006: Gaza Today, 12:30 p.m., local time

An Israeli Apache gunship launched its rockets three times against Palestinian civilians in the east of Gaza City. The target was an Islamic Jihad member, who was killed. But civilians were not spared—at least nine were killed, thirty-five injured, and the number of killed may increase due to the serious injuries. Two emergency health workers were killed trying to evacuate the injured.

I am writing from home, unable to focus, trying to reassure my youngest daughter, while F-16 jet fighters are crossing the sky. Electricity may be cut off any minute—this is the case after every attack. So I'm writing in a hurry.

Friends, neighbors, colleagues...my quick message to you: Israel has a free hand to attack us in Palestine with the full financial, political, and military support of the United States. Talk about democracy? Please, forget it. It is a world of one hopeless criminal power: the United States of America.

Together we shall do many things, the future is ours, one day we shall see a just peaceful world, and we shall prevail. I love you all.

June 13, 2006: Gaza Tonight

I am writing while Israeli jet fighters are in the sky, with their horrible sound, bringing death and horror. It is 10:30 p.m. Like everyone here, I am waiting, hoping they will not go ahead with their operation into Gaza. The outcome would be horrible. Resistance fighters are going ahead with their preparations too, but it is obvious which side will overwhelm the other. In any case, with resistance or no resistance, Israel attacks us all the time. Many civilians will be killed. I'm listening to the local radio, and it seems that the operation started in Khan Yunis. The artillery started shelling, under the cover of Apache gunships and jet fighters. I'm able to write now, but I don't know what will happen next, the power might be cut off soon. A few hours ago, Mohammed and Sondos, my dear kids, had a narrow escape on their way home. A car exploded some 150 meters from my house, one person killed and four injured. I cannot help but worry, I'm a mother after all.

I shall stay strong. Tomorrow at the Red Crescent office, we are supposed to get some medications for the emergency department of al-Awda hospital. The shipment was stopped at the closed border. I hope to get it through with the WHO's help. Not sure we shall receive them in time, but I shall keep trying.

The sound from the warplanes in the sky is getting louder. It is big relief for me to keep writing. I pray for the safety of all the children of the world, including Israel's children.

June 14, 2006: When Words Fail Me

These are difficult times for Palestinians, and particularly for Gazans. It's all the more difficult when I'm away and can do little more than watch my people from afar being bombarded and besieged. When words fail me, I always take comfort in the power of those who can convey our situation to the world.

Here are two quotes from two excellent articles by Danny Rubinstein and Gidon Levy:

> The events of this past weekend should not come as a surprise to anyone: The deterioration has been going on for weeks, and the question that should be asked is not what Israel is doing to counter the Qassams, but what it is not doing. An army that fires missiles at busy streets and tank shells at a beach cannot claim there was no intent to harm innocent civilians.
>
> —Gidon Levy

> As long as Israel does not announce a change of policy, a desire for a complete cease-fire, and a genuine willingness for dialogue—this is how the situation will continue.
>
> —Danny Rubinstein

There was also an interview on Amy Goodman's news program Democracy Now *with my aunt, Mona el-Farra—physician, community activist, and author of the blog "From Gaza, with Love"—which discusses, among other things, claims that the beach massacre was not the result of an Israeli shelling.*

June 27, 2006: Bracing for the Worst—Electricity Cut Off, Bridges Bombed, and Sonic Boom Attacks

Friends and family in Gaza have told me they are bracing themselves for the worst, while praying for the best. In Rafah, the refugee camp that has not been spared the wrath of the Israeli Army on so many occasions in the past and where 16,000 Palestinians have lost their homes to bulldozers, families have holed themselves indoors, fearing for their lives.

Israel has taken control of the border area, including the Rafah crossing and the airport. Colleague, friend, and activist Fida Qishta—with whom I toured the northeast United States—is on her way to Egypt, where she will have to remain until she is allowed by Israeli forces to enter her home in Rafah. They have sealed off the Gaza Strip in its entirety. I worry about her safety. I received a frantic telephone call from her from an airport in London where her flight was delayed. Meanwhile, journalist colleagues have told me that CNN and BBC crews from Jerusalem were not allowed through the Erez crossing into Gaza yesterday.

Israeli F-16s bombed Gaza's main bridge, right next to my father's farm, between northern and southern Gaza. They have also destroyed Gaza's only power plant, and electricity in most of Gaza has been cut off as a result. I've just spoken to my grandmother in Khan Yunis, who confirmed the entire Strip has plunged into darkness, with people stocking up on food and supplies. The electricity has also been cut off in hospitals and clinics. I'm not sure how long the generators can last.

Friends in Gaza City tell us that terrorizing sonic boom attacks—illegal in Israel, the United States, and most of the world—have resumed, stronger than before, full force, by low-flying jets breaking the sound barrier throughout the night over the civilian population.

June 28, 2006: Gaza under Large-Scale Military Attack

There's only a one-week supply of medications at al-Awda hospital. If the Israeli operations continue and casualties increase, a health disaster will follow.

1:30 a.m.: The Gaza bridge has been destroyed, jet fighters are still in the sky hitting many targets. The Gaza power plant was hit by at least seven missiles, I can see a big fire from my window and hear the sirens of emergency vans. The gunboats started shelling too; I live by the beach.

7:00 a.m.: Last night, it was very dangerous for me to reach the computer. Power was cut off. I stayed on the floor with my son and daughter. Like everyone else in Gaza, we didn't sleep at all. We couldn't due to the sonic booms from jet fighters constantly showering us—it is a very loud and horrifying sound.

July 1, 2006: I Am OK

I'm a representative of a just and noble cause. Nothing whatsoever will frighten me. My fellow friends are those who are resisting all kinds of injustices everywhere—including Palestine. I strongly believe in what Che Guevara said: "When you are shaking with anger, seeing injustice imposed on somebody, far away, then you are a comrade and a real human"—please, somebody help me to get the right phrase. What happened to the Jews and others during the Second World War is a shameful crime against humanity. And it is really awful and backward to judge people according to their color, race, or religion. We must all work together for a brighter future for all the children of the world.

I'm OK...I go through phases but will never surrender to despair.

July 1, 2006: Collective Punishment and State Terrorism

My friend Hoda lives next to the Hamas-controlled Palestinian Interior Ministry building in Gaza which was hit last night by Israeli rockets. The attack occurred at 1:00 a.m. or 2:00 a.m. Please forgive me for the inaccuracy, I'm starting to lose track of days and nights, and how many times we were attacked. Hoda told me that the whole building was shaking. She went out in her pajamas. All the residents were out in their nightwear, children were crying hysterically, and fumes filled the area. Next to the building that was targeted, a house where a family with six children lives was badly damaged. The fire brigade used Hoda's flat to put out the fire. The Interior Ministry building was empty during the attack! The aim was gratuitous revenge. I live some

150 meters from Hoda's place. Nobody is safe; no one is immune. What happened to Hoda reminded me of the night when Arafat's headquarters in Gaza were attacked two years ago—I lived too close, that night thirty-seven shells hit the building.

The power is still off. We had it for three hours yesterday, enough to recharge my laptop and mobile phone, and do some cooking. I'm highly concerned about the hospitals; fuel supply for local electricity generators is running low. The borders are completely sealed, and no fuel has been allowed into Gaza since the start of the Israeli attack. Medical supplies are running low too. We don't have enough supplies in reserve, because of previous ongoing sanctions. Our drugstores have been emptied. Water supply is scarce, so we need to ration it. We are going through a humanitarian disaster.

Sonic booms: when jet fighters break the sound barrier, it's a terrifying experience. They do it throughout the day and night. Many international human rights organizations have appealed to Israel to stop this horrific practice, because of its traumatic effect on people. They never used it before the withdrawal of Israeli settlers from Gaza.

How can I let you know what I experience during these sonic-boom raids? If I'm sleeping, my bed shakes violently, my daughter jumps into my bed trembling with fear, and then both of us end up on the floor. My heartbeat goes very fast, and I have to calm down my daughter. Now she knows we need to calm each other—she feels my fear. If I'm awake, I flinch and scream loudly, I can't help it. OK, I'm a medical doctor and an activist, but these sonic booms make me hysterical. We are all humans and have our own thresholds. The sonic booms also cause glass windows to break and crash down with a terrifying noise, and tin roofs in refugee camps collapse on people. After each sonic boom raid, the hospitals receive another batch of traumatized children.

Some 1.4 million residents in Gaza are subjected to *collective punishment*. Feelings of hate will only grow. All these assaults and savage aggressions against innocent people will bring neither peace nor security for Israel—only justice will.

Israel is talking about its citizens' security, against militiamen armed with crude homemade rockets. Israel is talking about terrorism. What can I call these sonic booms and the attack on Gaza's only power plant, but *state terrorism*?

July 5, 2006: Hoda's Building Is Hit Again, 1:45 a.m.

An explosion, very big and so loud. I'm fully awake and so is my daughter Sondos. We hardly can see anything in the dark. The drone hit the Interior Ministry building again, with one missile that completely destroyed the building. I contact my friend Hoda who lives next to the building. She is screaming hysterically, shouting in pain, trapped under broken windows. All the windows in her flat broke. Fumes fill the place, and she is waiting for the emergency team to evacuate her. I can hear her neighbors' hysterical screams over the phone. I feel helpless; I don't know what to do. I phone again to offer help, she says she is OK, but I know she is not.

I visited Hoda four hours ago. We were both tense. A third friend asked us to talk about anything but politics. We tried, but we couldn't. I left her and walked home, only five minutes from her place.

Sound from the warplanes is high in the sky. I can't go to Hoda's because I can't leave my daughter alone. I expect more air raids. I'm sure some other friends are there with her now, given she lives alone. While writing, I hear another explosion; they hit an empty school in another neighborhood.

I have no analysis. Maybe you can try to help me understand? Why hit an empty building twice? I see it as a desperate act to humiliate and intimidate. They will not succeed.

July 8, 2006: My Mother

I did not tell you before about my mother. She lives in Khan Yunis, twenty-two kilometers south of Gaza City. I was born there, and lived there until I was sixteen, when I left to go to the university in Egypt. My mother is eighty-four, living alone after my father's death, and she is physically disabled. But she is well looked after. My older sister lives next door to her, and I visit her twice weekly at least. Since the start of the Israeli "Summer Rain" Operation, I haven't been able to reach her. I was overwhelmed with the situation at the hospital. Plus, the two bridges connecting northern Gaza to Khan Yunis in the south were destroyed in the first few hours of the military assault. I was afraid to use the unreliable side roads, and I was not ready to risk leaving Sondos alone.

Nonetheless, my mother thinks I'm "Superwoman" and can do miracles. She kept phoning and asking me to visit her. My sister asked me not to risk it. But knowing the Israeli operation is now focused on northern Gaza, I decided to take the risk. My mother was grumpy, unsatisfied with my quick visit.

My mother is a retired head teacher. She has lived through all the stages of the Israeli-Palestinian conflict. She directly witnessed what happened in Palestine during the British mandate, and how Israel was founded on the ruins of the Palestinian people, uprooted from villages and towns that were later occupied by Jews from all over the world.

My mother remembers all this. She also remembers the Moses family, a Jewish family, who were my parents' friends, in Jaffa—or Haifa, I'm not sure. Next time I visit Mother I shall ask her.

July 10, 2006: Fishing Boats Subjected to Israeli Army Fire, 11:00 a.m.

There has been no electricity in my apartment for the last eighteen hours. I would like to quickly share with you what I have seen in front of my window in the last fifteen minutes. Gaza fishermen have not been allowed to go fishing since the start of the recent assault on Gaza. Fish is expensive and scarce. (Can you believe it—fish is expensive and scarce in a city on the sea like Gaza!?) Now is the season for the cheapest fish that most Gazans can afford, which is sardine—small and tasty, and very popular too. For the last two weeks fishing boats haven't been allowed into the sea.

Today I watched a desperate fishing boat, literally under my window, maybe 150 meters into the sea. All of a sudden, I heard heavy shelling and shooting. I asked Sondos to move to the back of the flat. With a quick glance I could see an Israeli gunboat firing at the fishing boat, forcing it back to the port. The boat was not hit, it was just a warning shot! I'm sorry I didn't tell you before about the suffering of the fishermen, and the farmers, workers, and students, all living under occupation.

July 14, 2006: From Bad to Worse—The Downpour Continues

Things are very bad in Gaza. Not to mention, things are also very bad in Lebanon, where Yassine's family lives—in the Wavel refugee camp in Baalbeck, a Hezbollah stronghold.

All of Lebanon is blockaded by air and sea, so Yassine has sort of become a double-refugee now: he can't go back to Palestine, nor Lebanon. It brings back very bad memories for him, having grown up during the civil war there, and narrowly escaping mass slaughter at the hands of Syrian-backed, Israeli-advised, Phalangists in the Tel Zaatar camp, where his family originally lived, and where his uncle went missing.

Of course, what's happening in Lebanon provides some uncertain relief for Gaza residents, where eighty-two Palestinians have been killed in the past twelve days, twenty-two of them children.

I was finally able to reach my aunt Mona who is doing an amazing job updating her blog under such duress, and who recently published an op-ed article in the Boston Globe *about the situation in Gaza. She was dazed and anxious, but had her wits about her. They had been without electricity for twenty-four hours when I spoke to her; people have been standing in long lines to purchase candles.*

And of course, Rafah is still closed. Eight people have died waiting to get home. Egypt, following Israeli orders, is refusing to open the gates.

The nights are turning into days, and days into nights, as the sonic booms shock them awake, shattering windows and terrorizing the population. The stress is taking its toll, but to quote my aunt: "though they are not living with ease, they are living with resolve."

Medicines are also running dangerously low. And to add to the misery, Israeli tanks have blockaded northern Gaza, where my aunt lives and where our house is, from southern Gaza, where my eighty-four-year-old grandmother lives on her own.

I think of them every day. I still cringe when I see in the news helicopters, or fireworks, or thunder. Today we had a thunderstorm, and the thunder was so loud it scared Yousuf [my son], who thought it was gunfire and shelling. As I tried to assure him he was safe, I wondered to myself, does safe have an address?

July 15, 2006: More than One Way to Get Home! (Alternatively: Of Love, Borders, and Desperation)

I've spoken a little in previous posts about the situation at the Rafah crossing—Gaza's only outlet to 1.4 million Palestinians. Israel has hermetically sealed it, along with other commercial crossings further north, since the end of June and the capture of the Israeli soldier. That move isolated over 2,000 Palestinians, including many elderly and sick people who go to Egypt to get treatments for cancers and other complicated illnesses that are unavailable in Gaza. Many thousands of others have been waiting in al-Arish, or Cairo, including my friend, and tragic bride, Yasmin. She flew in to Egypt to meet up with her fiancé, to travel together and be married with their families in Gaza. He arrived ahead of her in Gaza. In Egypt, she had to wait for her late luggage to arrive and was consequently sealed out. Now, he cannot get out, and she cannot get in. They missed their wedding date, of course, as she sits helplessly awaiting some good news that will allow her to reunite with her husband-to-be.

Included among those 2,000 Palestinians on the border is colleague and activist Fida Qishta, who I spoke with in New York and Connecticut earlier last month. She flew to Egypt and met up with her family—who had just left Gaza to meet up with her—at the border town, just when the border closed.

Yesterday, a group of armed Palestinians resorted to exploding a hole in the crossing to allow people through, including Fida. She emailed me today to let me know she made it through safely.

July 23, 2006

During my visit to a children's center in Nusseirat refugee camp, the sound of artillery shells being fired at the nearby AlMagazi refugee camp was loud. The girls inside the center took me around to see their arts and crafts activities. The most moving one was the dream tree, in which girls between the ages of eleven and fourteen expressed their dreams of safety, education, sports activities, reading good books, traveling, going to the seaside, visiting friends and relatives, having electricity and good drinking water, etc.

One of the girls said, "We will never give up dreaming. I dream of living in Jaffa where my family lived before 1948. My grandmother tells me how life was great in Jaffa and I dream of going back. Nobody can stop me from dreaming, nobody should take my dreams away."

The girls danced to the music of Palestinian folklore and I passed a message of love and solidarity from friends all over the world who believe that Palestinians have the right to live in dignity. Meanwhile, the Israeli artillery shelling continued.

As I started my journey back to Gaza City, a drone was in the sky and gunboats were patrolling the sea. Driving on the rough side road, I bypassed the destroyed bridges and the disabled power plant, and I thought of the drawings at the children's center of army tanks, dead and injured people, funerals, and masked men.

I dream of the day when I shall be able to see children's drawings of green spacious parks, meadows, sports activities, and a safe seaside.

July 26, 2006: Home Sweet Home… I Wonder, 6:45 p.m.

Al-Awda hospital emergency room. Shahd, an eight-month-old baby girl, and Maria, a four-year-old child, arrived at the hospital dead. Their mother Somia and her remaining two daughters arrived at the hospital suffering from serious injuries. The two girls are now in the operating room where doctors are trying hard to save their lives. The mother's injuries are very critical; she was referred to Gaza City's central hospital, Al Shifa, for treatment.

Samir, an extremely traumatized husband and father, was unable to believe what happened to his family. Early this evening an Israeli army tank launched a missile at this family's home inside Jabalia refugee camp where the Israelis are conducting a large-scale raid against both the camp and the eastern part of Gaza City.

This assault started in the early hours of the morning. At 4:00 a.m., loud explosions from the sea, air, and land woke me up along with everyone in Gaza City and Jabalia. I didn't know what was happening until I switched on my little battery-powered radio. The death toll reached twenty-four, a number that might increase. Dozens of injured are being sent to all of the town's different hospitals including Al-Awda in Jabalia.

Many homes were demolished, many places are hazardous to reach. The roads are deserted and the mood is anxiety and insecurity. Many children lost their parents, many parents lost their children. Our news isn't covered; people are feeling disappointed, devastated, and abandoned by the world's reaction, especially the governments.

Your solidarity is needed at these times. Please spread the truth. End the occupation! End the aggression against Palestinians and Lebanese!

July 28, 2006: Update from Gaza and Lebanon

It's difficult blogging from way over here. I feel impotent, a far-and-away observer, distant and a little too comfortable. And I don't like it.

News from back home: Yassine's parents were able to flee to Syria, where he has two aunts in refugee camps. His brother stayed behind in Baalbeck to guard their home, lest the refugee camps also become "accidental targets." His sister and her family are still in Tyre, and communication is on and off with them.

From Gaza: things are grim. We speak regularly with my father's cousin, who tells us that because of the closures, vegetables are being dumped on the local markets, with tomatoes selling for three shekels a box (less than a dollar). The problem is, there is no refrigeration and no electricity. This is the middle of the summer, so people can only buy what they can cook and eat the same day.

Another email from Fida about life in Rafah under siege: "Life here is awful, I can't believe it, is this Gaza? I can't even imagine what's going on. No one in the world to help or even feel what's going on. It's horrible...people every day killed and nobody says look at the Palestinians or Lebanese. The food, the water, the electricity, all of this awful. I came back with some money and I thought I will help a lot, but I gave them to some families and now I'm looking to these families and looking to my hands and there is nothing I can do...I came back and thought I can do something, but the Israelis destroyed more and killed more, and now in Rafah a lot live in the schools after they lost their houses."

July 29, 2006: Bad News

The mother I mentioned in my previous story didn't make it. She passed away three hours later, leaving behind her husband Samir and the two surviving daughters. One of the girls was seriously injured and is still at the hospital. Somia, the mother, was hanging the children's clothes at their home in Jabalia when she and her children were hit by the missile. Neighbors told me that the baby was next to the mom, in her carriage. I'm unable to visit the family. I have no words.

August 13, 2006: Rest in Peace, Um Fuad

Last year, while visiting Yassine's family in Baalbeck, I met Um Fuad. She was married in the year of the Nakba. Then a young girl, Um Fuad was separated from her husband when her village, Yajur of Akka, was attacked. She fled to Jordan, her husband to Lebanon. And for two years they lived apart.

"People would see me hanging laundry in the refugee camp there and come ask for my hand; they didn't realize I was already married, and those who did thought I had given up hope," she told me.

Eventually, two years later, he came for her, making his way across the border from Lebanon into Palestine, "infiltrating," since he was not allowed back to his village as a refugee, and from there to Jordan, where he asked around until he found her. She had taken him for dead, or at least thought he had abandoned her. Together, they sneaked back to Lebanon, where their families were.

Thirty-four years later, she was widowed. Abu Fuad and two of their sons were killed by an Israeli air strike on Baalbeck in 1984.

And now, fifty-eight years later, this second invasion had taken her. She sought refuge in Syria after Baalbeck was targeted a couple of weeks ago, living with hundreds of other Palestinian refugees in a public school.

Um Fuad died today, away from all of her remaining sons in Lebanon, a twice-over refugee, unable to return, or be buried, in her home in Yajur. Another story, another statistic, another "inconvenient" refugee. Um Fuad, dead at seventy-two.

May she rest in the peace she never found in her life.

August 13, 2006: Meanwhile, in Palestine

Homesickness is getting the best of us. My mother—who came to visit and is now along with my father stuck here with us—decided to ask if we could pick leaves to make mahshi waraq inab *[stuffed grape leaves]. So we did, nostalgically, remembering our little farm in central Gaza's Zawayda village, now bursting with unpicked, past their prime, plump seaside grapes.*

And later at home, we boiled them, and boiled some more—only to realize this particular variety was too fibrous for our mahshi. *Durham is no Gaza, I suppose. And Muscadine grapes are not Sheikh Ijleen's.*

Saddened, we stopped wrapping and called home. Our cousin gives us the latest. We learn that in July, the Israeli military killed 163 Palestinians in the Gaza Strip and "Summer Rain" continues. But the headlines here tell us that the days are "tragic" for Israel. Tragedy excludes us—our children are not children; a mother's tears are no tears at all; we are less human.

On the Lebanese front, Yassine's sister moved with her children and husband from Tyre, which has been heavily bombed in recent days, to Sidon. She is taking shelter in a place that has no doors or windows with forty other people.

So we drift, from one news report to the next, one phone call to the next, one story to the next, and nothing quite makes sense anymore. Unaligned and displaced, we carry on with our lives, not knowing quite what to do with ourselves, until Yousuf inevitably asks me, distressed:

"Mom, what is it?"
I respond, "Mom is sad, my dear."
"But why?"
"I have a booboo [wawa], my dear."
"Well then, go to the doctor!"

If only this wawa *had such a simple remedy.*

August 19, 2006: Young Voice from Jabalia Refugee Camp

I would like today to introduce to you Adam Khalil. You can learn more about him and about his life under occupation in the Jabalia refugee camp from his blog: http://nagyelali.blogspot.com.

I want to tell you how I got to know Adam. I started the Jabalia Library Project in 1992 in response to an initiative of Dr. Mounir Fashe, former director of Tamer Institute in Ramallah. Dr. Fashe launched a campaign to encourage reading inside the Palestinian community and I responded by setting up the library project next to the medical center in Jabalia where I work. The aim was to encourage youngsters to read and to provide them with books. At that time, Adam came along with other kids pleased to be part of this activity inside the camp. This modest project developed into a nice children's club with different activities, where the kids can read, dance, play, paint, learn English, and do other activities.

One goal of the project was to encourage kids to think in a democratic way and to give them a chance to read freely. We didn't try to tell them what they should and shouldn't read, we just provided them with a place of their own, distant from the poor crowded alleys of the camp, and the violence and atrocities of the Israeli occupation. Another goal was to encourage kids to be active members of their community, participating in its development, strengthening values of giving and sharing with others—to develop human resources in the community. The funds alone do not suffice, which were very scarce at the beginning in any case.

Many kids, including Adam, benefited from the project over the years. It started as a dream, then the dream became a reality because everybody was helping. The entire community helped, assisted by the uninterrupted efforts of the Union of Health Work Committees.

August 28, 2006: Fishing in Gaza

I live by the sea. I love the sea. When I was young I always thought of myself as a fish that cannot live outside its sea. I love swimming, and walking by the sea any time, but especially in the morning and at sunset. Now looking out of my window, watching the sea, and the fishing boats, fills my heart with pain and sadness—feelings I cannot describe. It is like a monster's hand getting hold of my heart, strong enough to crush it. I am resisting with all of my strength, but how long shall I stay strong and resist? I do not know, I cannot predict. All those thoughts crossed my mind while watching some fishing boats which sailed too close to the seashore. The shelling from the gunboats warned them to go back to the harbor. But it is not just warning, it is like pushing a herd of sheep, ordering it to go back to the port.

Since the Israeli army's latest assault against Gaza, fishing boats are not allowed to go to sea. A few take the risk of sailing close to the shore. But every time they are threatened by the warships' firing. Yesterday, one of the fishing boats was shelled by the warships, then set on fire and completely destroyed. The fishermen on board were not hurt as they jumped into the sea. The shooting continued all through the night, so continuous and close to my building that my daughter was frightened and I couldn't sleep. We both rested on the floor of my bedroom.

The fishing industry in Gaza has been paralyzed for the past eight weeks. Since the capture of the Israeli soldier, 3,000 fishermen are not allowed to go fishing, and 35,000 people who rely on this industry are jobless. There's no fish in the Gaza markets, though Gaza is famous for fish meals. Now we can have fish only in our dreams. Israel can never stop us from dreaming.

Tyre. Iman Hoballah from Chakra village finds refuge in Bass refugee camp. (*as-Safir*)

11

Nightmares: How Gaza Offends Us All

Jennifer Loewenstein

In leaked testimony to the Winograd Committee investigating Israel's mismanagement of the summer 2006 Lebanon war, Israeli prime minister Ehud Olmert admitted that the war had been carefully planned at least four months ahead of time, or by March 2006. Nonetheless Israel and the United States continue to maintain that the five-week-long war—in which more than a thousand Lebanese civilians were killed, thousands more maimed, hundreds of thousands displaced, and whole villages, neighborhoods, and the infrastructure of Lebanon destroyed—was a matter of "self-defense." Facts such as that Hezbollah fired no rockets into Israel until after Israel's savage aerial attacks on southern Lebanese villages had begun, or that Israel had left unresolved for years the bitter issues of Lebanese prisoners of war and the occupation of the Shebaa Farms region, only generate more questions when one considers how easily negotiations could have defused growing tensions.

We find disturbingly similar assertions and patterns of behavior by Israel regarding its forty-year-long occupation of the Palestinian territories, an occupation that has claimed tens of thousands of lives, the local economies, family homes, schools, clinics, farms, agricultural land, resources, and entire regional infrastructures. In this, the occupation threatens to destroy the very fabric of Palestinian society. Why, we must ask ourselves, has Israel—with the all-embracing support and encouragement of the United States—been allowed to pursue such reckless and destructive regional policies? Indeed, in the case of occupied Palestine, we see a weak, oppressed, and effectively defenseless people repeatedly and brutally assaulted, and yet perversely portrayed as the quintessential regional menace threatening Israel's very survival.

Israel has become an offshore U.S. military base, stockpiling the most technologically advanced, state-of-the-art weaponry in the world—including arsenals of nuclear, biological, and chemical weapons capable of wreaking massive destruction on any power by which it might feel threatened. Nevertheless, Israel has managed to represent itself successfully as the beleaguered and besieged outpost in a dangerous and inhospitable frontier land. As its onslaught against Lebanon intensified in viciousness day after day during the summer of 2006, with mounting atrocities recorded on film and in the press, the Gaza Strip languished unseen under repeated assaults on its citizens and their surroundings. When the war in Lebanon finally ended, Western eyes again focused their attention elsewhere—satisfied that the most recent Middle Eastern calamity had concluded. But in fact, it continued unabated in Gaza, and it continues each day with barely a word uttered in protest.

In early November, Israel conducted yet another "operation" in Gaza, this time against the citizens of Beit Hanoun. Spokesman for the Israeli Ministry of Foreign Affairs Mark Regev stood in front of TV cameras telling the world yet again that its massacre of civilians in this impoverished village was a matter of "self-defense." Once again Israel, which has been allowed to create and exacerbate an unacceptable occupation with all of its attendant ills, insists that any reaction against that occupation justifies its continuation. Silence and indifference to the Palestinian cause have, at least in the short run, practically assured its defeat. Preparations for the next war against Lebanon, now in the making, could change all of this as victims of the relentless injustices excused repeatedly and resolutely by the United States come to make common cause with each other across the region.

A slightly different version of this essay was posted on the CounterPunch *website on November 9, 2006.*

—Jennifer Loewenstein

November 2006

An open jaw with yellowed teeth gaped out of its bloodied shroud. The rest of the head parts were wrapped in a plastic bag and placed atop the jaw and nostrils, as if to be close to the place where they once belonged. The bag was red from the pieces that were stuffed inside it. Below the jaw was a slit-open human neck—a fleshy, wet wound smiling pink and oozing out from the browned skin around it, the neck that was still linked to the body below it. Above him, in the upper freezer of the morgue lay a dead woman, her red hennaed hair visible for the first time to strange men around her. More red plastic was wrapped around an otherwise absent chin. She died demonstrating outside a mosque in Beit Hanoun—in northern Gaza, where more than sixty men sheltered during the artillery onslaught by Israeli tanks and cannons.

Most of the others still had their faces intact. They lay on their silver morgue trays, stiff as frozen food. One man had a green Hamas band tied around his head; he looked like a shepherd from some forgotten pastoral age. Another's eyes were partially opened, his face looking out in horror as if he'd died seeing it coming. Then there was a muddy, grizzled blob on the bottom-left tray, black curls tangled and damped into its rounded head and blessedly shut eyes. A closer look revealed a child, a boy of four: Majed was outside playing important childhood games when death came in like thunder and rolled him up in a million speckles of black mud.

Muslim burials take place quickly. This is a godsend to the doctors, nurses, and undertakers who, at the hospitals and morgues, desperately need the space for the next batch of casualties who would sleep on the same sheets and steel-framed beds, in the same humid heat, in the same close, crowded, grief-stricken rooms, often on the floors with the same tired, unpaid attendants doing their rounds without the proper supplies to help the victims who were still alive. Some would die on the operating table, like the young man gone now to the Kamal Adwan hospital morgue when his wounds became too much for his body to bear. Two little girls preceded him earlier the same day. Blessed are those who leave this human wasteland washed and shrouded for a quiet, earthy grave.

Today is November 8, 2006; the hospitals will be filled beyond capacity again when the scores of wounded and 18 civilian dead—women, men, and children blasted out of their sleep into human chunks—from a pre-dawn attack on Beit Hanoun are rolled out of the ambulances and into the freezers of Shifa or Kamal Adwan hospitals in the northern Gaza Strip. How dare they sleep in their houses at night when the tanks are barking out commands: a dead mother lying face down, her two dead children each wrapped in one of her arms underneath her, blocked the road where they once walked, like barriers at a checkpoint.

Do you believe this was an accident? That an international investigation will ever take place? Like after Jenin? Like after Dan Halutz and his 2,000-pound bomb dropped on an apartment building in Gaza City just after midnight on a hot July night killing fifteen people, nine of them women and children? Like after the siege of Jabalya in the fall of 2004? Like after "Operation Rainbow" in Rafah? Like after Huda Ghalia's family was blasted into nothingness during an outing on a Gaza beach? Will U.S. eyes, glued to their TV screens to find out which marketed candidate won the corporate-managed midterm elections, ever know that yet another massacre of Palestinians took place?

At Shifa Hospital, Gaza's central hospital, Dr. Juma Saqa and his staff cope with the daily shortages of supplies, such as kidney dialysis machines, fans, and clean linens; cancer medications are unavailable to the increasing number of cancer patients; and elective surgeries such as for hernias or tonsils are a thing of the past. This is where doctors and nurses witness how the water that Gazans drink causes innumerable ailments—rotting teeth, anemia in children, and kidney dysfunction—because of its brackish, poisonous quality. This is where children lie half-naked in their beds, with white tape across their noses holding tubes to their faces so that they may eat or breathe—like three-year-old Ahmad, also from Beit Hanoun, who took a bullet in the right side of his belly that exited on the left. His mother stands over him passively, grateful. Ahmad, at least, is going to live. But for what?

Those first nights in November, explosions sounded in the northeastern corner of Gaza City: a succession of bullets, booms, bombs, and artillery fire. On the first night of the onslaught we could still see lights from Beit Hanoun, ten miles from us, blinking and twinkling as if nothing were really happening; it was all a dream—fireworks, a distant celebration perhaps. But then, by the second night only a swath of blacked-out space lay in the place of Beit Hanoun, now without electricity or water, as the booms continued unabated for an hour or more. The pilotless drones circled round again and again—above Beit Hanoun and Gaza; automated people-monitors taking stock of the activity below. Nobody from Beit Hanoun could leave by day to get to work without announcing to the tanks and the drones that he was prepared to sacrifice his life for a semblance of normalcy. All men between the ages of sixteen and thirty-five were rounded up onto trucks and hauled away for "questioning." What will happen to them and their families? Will anyone follow up? Will they add to the 10,000-plus Palestinian prisoners in Israeli jails, left to rot while their wives, children, sisters, brothers, and parents go on struggling to survive?

There lies Gaza, stretched twenty-eight-miles long in a tumbledown, graying, decaying heap of debris: yawning, tired, wretched, full of garbage. Tape gauze over your nose to avoid the smell of sewage and burning trash. Try not to notice the metal-shuttered shopfronts, the half-empty stores, and the stands with rotting produce for sale. Pay no heed to the rats scurrying along the alleyways of the camps, content to cohabitate with humans in the same giant trash bins. Ignore the proliferation of horse- and donkey-carts clopping along the streets for lack of fuel, the ribs of the tired beasts jutting out from their bellies as boys whip them along to keep them going. The cerulean-blue sky illuminating the crumbling city, the sea sparkling up against littered sands, the palm trees and bougainvillea radiant in the November sun appear like dramatic non sequiturs on this lurid stage. Like the box of brightly wrapped chocolates offered to the journalists filming the woman's wounded son on the hospital bed as she cries out her frustrations and horror at the Americans and the Israelis who are killing her family, "Why?", she asks. Why, why, why?

Ask Mark Regev, Israel's eager, hideously sincere government spokesperson. On CNN's international news he tells us in earnest that this is Israeli self-defense. The Qassam fire into Sderot and Ashkelon must stop, but not the tank fire or missiles into the homes of a million and a half hostages in the Strip. *Israelis* have the right to defend themselves. The "operation" in Beit Hanoun will not stop until the Qassams stop. Each word is driveled out of his mouth into a bubble of obscenity for everyone watching from the vantage point of Gaza. Verbal pornography, sadomasochistic jargon from the prince of Hasbara leaks onto the dust like poisonous bile sought after, bought, and paid for by the lords of power and their occupying machinery.

The shoddy, homemade Qassams hiss like alley cats when they are fired into the skies: the latest gift to the Israeli overlords seeking more excuses to destroy Palestine. Stupid and bestial, these glorified pipe bombs zing across the border like crazed beasts not knowing where they are going. They'll dart forever like this until the occupation ends. The Gazans know this, Hamas knows it, Fatah knows it, the Popular Front for the Liberation of Palestine knows it; in Israel, Labor and Likkud know it, Meretz knows it, Yisrael Beiteinu knows it, Shas knows it, Peretz knows it, Olmert knows it, Lieberman knows it, Sharon knew it, and the Israeli people know it; and the leaders of America know this. So, forty years after 1967, and fifty-eight years after 1948, why is the occupation not yet over?

Because Israel does not want it to end. Because Israel wants the land and the resources without the people. Because you have to eviscerate a society in order to maintain total control over it. Because the United States says that's just fine with us, you serve our purpose well: you want regional hegemony and global deference? Do our bidding and we will look the other way. You help make the "war on terror" convenient. Together we will wreck Lebanon, smashing any deterrent capability on our way to Tehran. Wait until the Syrians see what's coming. Help fit Iraq into our scheme; we'll fill our coffers with oil profits, heavy investment, and corporate concessions. Who will ever know about the slums of Beirut or the peasants of the Bekaa? Who the hell cares about a million and a half poverty-stricken Gazans and their dust, their sand, their stinking, crumbling heap of a homeland?

Leaving Gaza at 6:30 a.m. on a bright Saturday morning, I hear a loud explosion. My cabdriver picks me up and we drive down the main street in Gaza City, in the direction of the Erez crossing. Suddenly, unexpectedly, there is a smoldering mass of wreckage in front of me, a melted car surrounded by boys picking at its still-hot exterior. Inside are four blackened, seared human shapes, faceless from the burns, charcoaled with shreds of steaming cloth visible from the road, and the smell of cooked human flesh. Sirens sound in the distance. Burnt and vaporized metal looks like what you see in a science fiction movie. Burnt humans look like singed papier mâché monsters whose pieces fall off at the hint of a breeze.

Gaza is sorry for these indiscretions, this poor taste, this unseemly topic of conversation. You are right to express your indignation. How dare Gaza speak of these things. But it is unable to conceal its secrets even with the blockade of goods and visitors in place; its voice is shrill, angry, and defiant even when muted through the layers of media deceit. It rises up through the lies like the smoke after each missile strike, the evidence of an unacceptable crime; a nightmare still unfolding.

Sabra-Shatila Camp. Children posing in one of the alleys.
(photo by Carol Chomsky)

12

An Arab Perspective on the "New Middle East"

Fawwaz Traboulsi

This essay is based on a translation of two articles that appeared (in Arabic) in the Beirut daily as-Safir *on two different dates, September 16 and October 10, 2006. Here they are combined into a single essay with minor modifications.*

The "New Middle East"—What's in a Name?

Every time U.S. policy-makers find themselves in dire straits in the Middle East, they come up with a new name for the region. There is no need to dwell on what has become an alarming habit to create and manipulate national identities in this part of the world according to the West's changing geostrategic interests and plans. Let's only recall a few stages in this history.

At the onset of the Cold War, our region's name changed from "Near East" to "Middle East" in order to incorporate Turkey, Iran, and Pakistan into pacts opposed to the Soviet Union. The most prominent and short-lived of these was the Baghdad Pact. This designation lost some of its currency with the rise of the Arab liberation movements that imposed "Arab World" as a common name for both the Mashriq (the eastern part of the Arab World) and the Maghrib (its western part).

The end of the Cold War revived the earlier name "Middle East," coupled with persistent efforts to replace "Arab World" with "Mena Region," the latter being an acronym for Middle East and North Africa. Thus, from now on, if we were asked about our identity, we shouldn't perhaps forget to say we are Mena-ian or from the Mena Region, rather than Arab!

After the Cold War and the floating of proposals for a peaceful settlement of the Israeli-Arab conflict, the signs of a "New Middle East" (yet another name!), centered around Israel and dominated by it, appeared in a book by Shimon Peres containing a whole program of highly ambitious if not utopian economic and developmental projects. However, in the aftermath of September 11, 2001, the war in Afghanistan and the invasion of Iraq, they dropped "New" from our region's name and preferred the term "area." They thus bestowed on us the new designation of "*Wider Middle East*" or "*Greater Middle East*," which in addition to the Arab countries of the Mashriq, included Israel, Iran, Pakistan, and Afghanistan.

The problem with such repeated renaming is that, as soon as we start getting used to a new name, those responsible for producing it proceed to replace it with something else. And every new designation for our region will sound emptier and more confusing than the previous one. Only a few years went by before "Wider" or "Greater" was dropped, and we found ourselves back again with "New" as the preferred qualifier for Middle East. The U.S.-Israeli war on Lebanon in the summer of 2006 revived the designation of "New Middle East" once more, which Condoleezza Rice offered us when she proclaimed this war was part of the "birth pangs of the New Middle East."

What's "New" in this New Middle East?

Is it the burying of the peace process in Palestine by reoccupying most of the West Bank, killing any prospect for a Palestinian state, and refusing to withdraw from the Golan Heights? Or is it the presence of two Arab camps competing over an illusion of bilateral solutions and failed plans? A Saudi-Egyptian-Jordanian axis is seeking to keep the status quo which is nothing but a means to preserve despotic regimes ridden with corruption and exploitation. This is a status quo whose central goal is the protection of Israel's borders and the elimination of instability surrounding it, be it in Lebanon or in Palestine. Facing the Saudi-Egyptian-Jordanian axis, we see a Syrian regime that viewed the war on Lebanon as an opportunity to engage in bilateral solutions by offering the United States special favors, which the Syrian minister of communications enumerated as follows in *al-Sahafa* newspaper on July 24, 2006:

- Assisting the United States in locating positions of the al-Qaeda organization in Lebanon. (We were under the impression that Lebanon, not the United States, should be the first to receive such assistance, as dictated by mutual defense and security arrangements between Syria and Lebanon!)

- Getting ready to play the role of a broker between the United States and Iran. (We were repeatedly told that there was a strategic alliance between Syria and Iran!)
- Last but not least, playing an "important role" in Iraq.

We are entitled to ask: All of this barter in exchange for what?

There is indeed something *new* in the New Middle East: the United States has put an end to the pretense of promoting democracy in this region. It has done so not only by refusing to recognize the victory of Hamas in the Palestinian legislative elections, but also by tolerating Israel's proclaimed intention to assassinate an elected prime minister (Ismail Hanieh of Hamas) on the pretext that Israel has the right to protect itself; by distorting the results of the Iraqi legislative elections; by sanctioning the sham of the Egyptian presidential elections; and by turning a blind eye on the renewal of a presidential mandate in Yemen that preceded and obviated the actual presidential elections. Not to speak of the bargains between the United States and the family-based and oil-based dictatorial regimes that fear their own populations and obtain what they can of their legitimacy from the United States to the detriment of their peoples.

Perhaps the *new* in this Middle East is the accelerated slide into civil warfare in Iraq, where the United States continues nourishing ethnic and sectarian fragmentations that can only serve to extend an occupation that it no longer knows how to escape or to pursue?

What is *new* is the Bush administration's determined efforts to disarm Hezbollah in pursuit of a victory that will reverse a dismal record of continuing failures and destruction in the region, which includes an obvious stalemate in the campaign against al-Qaeda and fruitless efforts in "the war on terror."

What is *new* is that the United States and Israel, after their war of July-August 2006, have not succeeded yet in imposing their conditions on Lebanon and the U.S.-dictated priorities of the "international community," including the disarming of Hezbollah and implementation of UN Security Council Resolution 1559!

As for Lebanon's "fragile democracy," which Bush has proclaimed his ardent desire to defend, Israeli wanton bombardments only managed to undermine it. Nor did the Judas kiss, which Condoleezza Rice planted on the cheek of Prime Minister Fuad Siniora, help in any way—God only knows if that was her message, that the Lebanese people will have to suffer on the cross for the weeks and months ahead.

Moderation, Not Democracy

All that is left for U.S. Secretary of State Condoleezza Rice is to add to her titles that of general secretary of the Arab League. For that was the role she played during the summit of "moderate Arabs" represented by the foreign ministers of the six Gulf states (Bahrain, Kuwait, Oman, Qatar, Saudi Arabia, and the United Arab Emirates) in addition to Egypt and Jordan. The summit was held in Cairo to address an agenda and division of responsibilities that Rice had partly revealed in a prior press conference in Jeddah.

Even without full disclosure and analysis of its deliberations, we can safely say that the Cairo summit pointed to a new approach that is being tested by Rice, namely, the implementation of American policies by means of the bloc of "moderate Arabs" that emerged during the most recent U.S.-Israeli war on Lebanon.

It was no coincidence that this new testing phase dealt a deathblow to remaining illusions about the U.S. campaign to spread democracy in the region. The priority is now for *moderation*, be it at the expense of *democracy* or even against it. In answer to a journalist's question about the shift from democracy to moderation, Rice responded that "moderate forces will ultimately become moderate democratic forces."

This admission that the forces of "Arab moderation" are not democratic does not need much elaboration, as it came straight from the horse's mouth, as the saying goes. Yet here are some other feats of the moderate Arabs:

- Moderate are the rulers whose hostility towards Iran for its uranium-enriching program to produce nuclear energy exceeds their hostility towards Israel with its two hundred to three hundred nuclear warheads.

- Moderate are those who are satisfied with the best terms offered by multinational oil corporations to exploit their oil resources as much as they are satisfied with investing the returns from these resources in the West.

- Moderate are those who welcome the presence of American military bases on their soil and do not oppose the use of these bases for shipping "smart bombs" to Israel during the recent war on Lebanon.

- Moderate are those who rule by means of armed militias that are exempt from international condemnation as long as they do not fight the U.S. occupation of Iraq and do not fire at Israel with as much as flowers.

- Moderate are those who do not make a big fuss when "democratic" and "moderate" Israel arrests the majority of the elected Hamas legislators in the Palestinian parliament, while those same moderates scream out loud against the "adventurism" of the Lebanese resistance when it captures Israeli soldiers to seek the release of Lebanese prisoners and liberate remaining Lebanese lands.

This does not mean that the "non-moderates" are necessarily democratic. It rather means that "moderation," which is another name for submission to the dictates of the American empire, will not give birth to democracy, neither now or ever.

It is now incumbent on pan-Arab nationalists of various stripes, Islamists, and even some leftists, to free themselves of the illusion that the United States has a vested interest in imposing democracy on them, as they go on voicing their opposition to U.S. actions. Unless their proclaimed opposition to U.S. policies is in fact an opposition, witting or unwitting, to democracy itself!

Sabra-Shatila camp. Carol Chomsky with schoolchildren.

Postscript

"We will take Lebanon twenty years back."

—Israeli chief-of-staff General Dan Halutz, July 12, 2006, quoted in a statement by Israeli Channel 10 television.

"The claim that we have lost is unfounded. Half of Lebanon is destroyed. Is that a loss?"

—Israeli prime minister Ehud Olmert, September 4, 2006, when challenged in a Knesset debate that the Israeli onslaught on Lebanon had not achieved its goals.

"I was damn proud of what we did."

—U.S. Ambassador John Bolton, March 22, 2007, in an interview for the BBC Radio 4 documentary *The Summer War in Lebanon*, when asked about the wisdom of the American position to prevent a ceasefire and to let the Israeli bombing campaign continue unchecked for five weeks.

"Beirut's genius was that it responded immediately to our needs as Arabs in an Arab world already gone repressive, drab, and insufferably mediocre. For some years one could, in Beirut, burn with a hard, gemlike flame; even the city's vice and profligacy had a brilliance you could not see elsewhere. The main consolation of these dark times is the sentiment that since Beirut once rose from obscurity it might again reappear from out of its catastrophic destruction..."

—Edward W. Said, from the Postscript of his book *After the Last Sky* (Pantheon, 1986), in words no less relevant today than they were twenty years ago.

We stand together to reaffirm a vision of hope—against the agents of war and destruction—for a Beirut that will rise again from its catastrophic destruction to come to terms with its past and embrace all its citizens. A Beirut, born of the Mediterranean sun, that will remain a haven for artists and writers, dissidents and political outcasts, and all who dare to think against the grain.

Timeline: Key Historical Dates in Relation to Lebanon

1920s The modern state system of the Middle East is established, after the defeat and dismembering of the Ottoman Empire in the First World War. The San Remo Conference grants mandates under the League of Nations to Britain and France for the administration of former Ottoman-ruled lands of the Middle East. The areas of present-day Lebanon and Syria are put under French rule, and the districts of present-day Palestine/Israel, Jordan, and Iraq under British rule. In Lebanon, French colonial authorities pursue a policy of apportioning government positions according to religious affiliations; this power-sharing formula becomes known as "confessionalism" (from the French *confession*, or "religious denomination").

1943 November: the Lebanese Parliament terminates the French mandate. France retaliates by dissolving the Lebanese Parliament and arresting the Lebanese president, prime minister, and several ministers. Under mounting internal and external (mainly from Britain and the United States) pressure, France relents and grants formal independence to Lebanon.

1948 May: the State of Israel is established. The "first Arab-Israeli war" leads to the uprooting of more than half of Palestine's native population, close to 800,000 people; the vast majority of Palestinians are displaced to the Gaza Strip, Jordan, Syria, and Lebanon.

1940s and 1950s The former Anglo-French colonial order in the Middle East weakens and gradually crumbles, undermined by both the emerging power of the United States after the Second World War and various nationalist movements demanding an end to foreign domination. Lebanon, Syria, Iraq, and Jordan acquire formal independence from their colonial rulers. The Middle East emerges as the major oil-producing region in the world and gains a new geostrategic importance.

1956 July 26: Egypt nationalizes the Suez Canal. October 30: Britain and France, in collusion with Israel, respond by attacking Egypt militarily. British and French troops invade the Suez Canal region; Israel, in its "second Arab-Israeli war," occupies the Sinai peninsula. The United States demands the withdrawal of all invading armies from Egyptian territory, which was completed by early 1957.

1958 May–June: armed revolt against pro-Western Lebanese president Camille Chamoun marks the "first Lebanese civil war." July 14: republican coup in Baghdad abolishes pro-

Western monarchy. July 15: U.S. marines land in Lebanon. An understanding between the U.S. and Egyptian governments allows for the election of Fouad Shihab as Lebanese president in succession to Camille Chamoun. October: U.S. marines leave Lebanon.

1967 June 5–11: "third Arab-Israeli war," the Six-Day War. Israel occupies the West Bank, the Gaza Strip, the Golan Heights of Syria, the Sinai peninsula of Egypt, and the Shebaa Farms of Lebanon. New displacement of Palestinian refugees into Jordan and Lebanon.

1968 First Palestinian commandos of the Palestine Liberation Organization (PLO) enter Lebanese territory.

1969 November 3: Cairo Agreement between the Lebanese government and the PLO allows the latter to keep its arms and conduct commando operations from southern Lebanon.

1970 Black September: bloody confrontation between PLO commandos and the Jordanian army. The result is the gradual erosion of the presence of the PLO in Jordan, forcing it to move its headquarters to Lebanon.

1973 October 6–26: "fourth Arab-Israeli war," also called the October War.

1975 April 13: a bus carrying Palestinians is ambushed by right-wing Phalangist militiamen in the Ayn al-Rummana district of Beirut, marking the beginning of the civil war. Fighting spreads to other parts of Lebanon, pitting an array of right-wing, mostly Christian, militia and parties—who are antagonistic to an armed Palestinian presence in Lebanon—against the broad coalition of the Muslim-leftist Lebanese National Movement (LNM) led by Kamal Jumblat, which consisted of several opposition parties generally supportive of the PLO.

1975–1990 The "second Lebanese civil war" extends over a period that includes Israeli occupation of a buffer zone along its border with Lebanon (1978), and Israeli invasion of Lebanon to evict PLO forces and install a Phalangist Lebanese president (1982).

1976 Several districts in and around Beirut, mostly populated by Palestinian refugees, poor Lebanese, and migrants from Syria and elsewhere, are attacked and destroyed by the Phalangists and their allies—Dbayyeh (January 13); Quarantine and Maslakh (January 20); and Tall al-Za'tar and Nab'a (August 12). Supported by the PLO, the LNM responds by attacking and evicting right-wing militias from several of their strongholds—Damour (January 22) and Beirut's hotel district (March 22). May: Syrian troops enter Lebanon through the northern and eastern borders to block advances of joint LNM-PLO forces against pro-government right-wing militias. Syrian intervention is facilitated by U.S. special envoy Dean Brown; Syria thus becomes a party in the Lebanese civil war and a major power broker in Lebanese internal affairs, shifting its support from one protagonist to another depending on regional and international circumstances.

1977 March 16: assassination of LNM leader Kamal Jumblat allegedly on directives from the Syrian government. November 19–21: Egypt's president Anwar al Sadat visits Jerusalem.

1978 March 14–15: in Operation Litani, the Israeli army invades southern Lebanon and establishes a buffer zone with an auxiliary local force, the South Lebanon Army (SLA), which is officered by former members of the Lebanese army. September: Camp David Accords between Egypt and Israel.

1979 January: Islamic revolution in Iran overthrows the Shah's regime. March: Sadat and Israeli prime minister Menachem Begin sign Egyptian-Israeli peace treaty in Washington, D.C.

1982 June 6: Israel launches Operation Peace of the Galilee, the "fifth Arab-Israeli war," also called Israel's "first Lebanon war." Israeli troops invade areas in southwestern Lebanon and besiege Beirut, resulting in the death of at least 17,000 Lebanese and Palestinians. Syrian troops retreat to northern Lebanon and the eastern Biqa' valley. August 23: Phalangist leader Bashir Gemayel elected Lebanese president; PLO troops evacuated from Lebanon by U.S.-led Multinational Force (MNF). September 14: Assassination of Bashir Gemayel. September 15: Israeli troops enter Beirut. September 15–17: Sabra and Shatila massacres. September 16: communist groups of the LNM launch the Lebanese National Resistance Front (LNRF) against Israeli occupation. By the end of the year, the PLO establishes its new headquarters in Tunis.

1984 MNF leaves Beirut. Official declaration of the creation of Hezbollah, already active in the resistance against Israeli occupation in southern Lebanon since 1982.

1987 December: the Palestinian Intifada ("uprising") starts in Israeli-occupied territories, called the "first Intifada" to distinguish it from the "al-Aqsa Intifada" of September 2000, and lasts until approximately 1990.

1989 October 22: the Lebanese Parliament convenes in Taif (Saudi Arabia) and issues Charter of National Concord to end civil war.

1990 In spite of the Taif Accords, fighting lingers between factions of the Lebanese civil war. August: Iraq invades Kuwait; Syria joins U.S.-led coalition against Iraq and is given green light to pacify Lebanon. October 1990: Syrian troops assault Lebanese presidential palace to evict interim prime minister Michel Aoun, who then takes refuge in French embassy and is allowed to depart for exile in France in August 1991.

1991 Syrian troops begin disarming Lebanese militias in accordance with Taif Accords, including groups of the LNRF resisting Israeli occupation, but Hezbollah remains defiant and refuses to disarm until all Lebanese soil is liberated.

1993 July 25: Israeli forces, hoping to pressure the Lebanese government to intervene against Hezbollah, launch a week-long attack against southern Lebanon, named Operation Accountability, forcing a new wave of Lebanese and Palestinian refugees to flee north. August–September: Oslo Accords between the PLO and the government of Israel. Pursuant to the Accords, the Palestinian National Authority (PNA) is established in May 1994 and headquartered in Ramallah since December 1995.

1996 April: Israel launches large-scale military attack on southern Lebanon in Operation Grapes of Wrath. Israeli military bombards UN base in the town of Qana killing more than 100 civilian refugees. The campaign fails in destroying the resistance spearheaded by Hezbollah and allied groups.

2000 May 25: Israeli troops withdraw from southern Lebanon, except from the Shebaa Farms and surrounding area, abandoning the buffer zone established in 1978, and leaving remnants of the SLA (the surrogate Lebanese militia) to their fate. September: the second Palestinian uprising starts in Israeli-occupied territories, called "al-Aqsa Intifada."

2001 September 11: Coordinated attacks by nineteen terrorists affiliated with al-Qaeda on the World Trade Center in New York City and the Pentagon in Arlington County, Virginia.

2003 March 18: The United States and its allies start invasion of Iraq.

2004 September 2: UN Security Council Resolution 1559, sponsored by the United States and France, calls upon Syria to end its military presence in Lebanon and for the disbanding and disarmament of all Lebanese and non-Lebanese militias in Lebanon.

2005 February 14: former Lebanese prime minister Rafiq Hariri is assassinated. March 8: Hezbollah and allied parties lead a massive demonstration in downtown Beirut against Western interference. March 14: pro-Western parties hold a massive counterdemonstration in downtown Beirut, led by various groups allied with Rafiq Hariri. April 25: mounting international pressure and popular Lebanese opposition force the complete withdrawal of Syrian troops from Lebanon. May–June: parliamentary elections lead to formation of a new council of ministers headed by Fuad Siniora, a close associate of Rafiq Hariri.

2006 January 25: Hamas wins a majority of seats in the elections for the Palestinian Legislative Council (PLC), giving it a mandate to form a new government to succeed the Fatah-led governments that dominated the PNA since it was established in 1994, pursuant to the Oslo Accords. The United States, Israel, and their European allies start a systematic campaign to undermine the new Hamas-led government and goad the Fatah opposition to challenge its authority in repeated armed confrontations. June 28: Israel launches a military attack on Gaza, named Operation Summer Rain. July 12: Israel opens military campaign against Lebanon in the "sixth Arab-Israeli war," also named Israel's "second Lebanon war." August 11: UN Security Council Resolution 1701 calls for an immediate cessation of hostilities and an international embargo on supplying arms to Hezbollah. August 14: Partial ceasefire comes into effect in Lebanon. Israeli military operations continue unabated in Gaza.

Contributors

Carol Chomsky, Noam's wife, doubles as road manager on his lecture tours. She accompanied him to Lebanon in May 2006. Some of her photographs from the trip are included in this book.

Noam Chomsky is Institute Professor Emeritus of Linguistics at the Massachusetts Institute of Technology, where he has been on faculty since 1955. He has written and lectured widely on linguistics, philosophy, international affairs, and other topics. His most recent books are *Failed States* and *Perilous Power* (with Gilbert Achcar and Stephen Shalom).

Mona el-Farra is a medical doctor by training and a co-founder of al-Awda hospital, located in the Jabalia refugee camp in the Gaza Strip. Currently, Mona is a health consultant, a community organizer, and a human-rights activist.

Laila el-Haddad is a journalist who, because of her profession, travels frequently. When not traveling, Laila divides her time between the United States, where her husband Yassine works, and Gaza, where her parents live.

Irene L. Gendzier writes on U.S. foreign policy in the Middle East. The second edition of her book, *Notes from the Minefield: United States Foreign Policy in Lebanon and the Middle East 1945–1958,* is out with a new Preface (New York: Columbia University Press, 2006); she also co-edited *Crimes of War: Iraq,* with R. Falk and R. J. Lifton (New York: Nation Books, 2006). She is currently Professor of Political Science and History at Boston University.

Assaf Kfoury is a mathematician, computer scientist, and political activist. He is an Arab American who grew up in Beirut and Cairo, and returns frequently to the Middle East. He is currently Professor of Computer Science at Boston University.

Jennifer Loewenstein is the Associate Director of the Middle Eastern Studies Program at the University of Wisconsin-Madison. She has lived and worked in Gaza City, Jerusalem, and Beirut and has written and lectured extensively on topics related to the Middle East.

Hanady Salman is the managing editor of the Lebanese newspaper *as-Safir*. She was born in Beirut in 1968 and lived in Paris between 1981 and 1986 after being forced to leave Lebanon during the civil war. She received her B.A. in Political Science from the American University in Beirut and her Master's Degree in Arab Politics from Georgetown University in 1997.

Rasha Salti is an independent curator and freelance writer. Trained as a printmaker, she earned a graduate degree in Liberal Studies from the Graduate Faculty at the New School for Social Research in New York City, in 2000. Her essays, articles, and chronicles have been published in Arabic and English, in publications such as: *al-Ahram Weekly* (Egypt); *Zawaya* (Lebanon); *The Jerusalem Quarterly Report* (Palestine); *Naqd* (Algeria); MERIP (USA); and *Bidoun* (USA).

Fawwaz Traboulsi is a historian, journalist, and longtime political activist. He is currently Professor of Politics and Social Studies at the Lebanese American University in Beirut, Lebanon. His most recent book in English is *A History of Lebanon* (London: Pluto Press, 2007).

Notes

1. Noam and Carol Chomsky in Beirut

1. Noam Chomsky's response to columnist Geov Parrish of the *Seattle Weekly,* January 18, 2006.

2. The lecture on May 9, entitled "The Great Soul of Power," was the first Edward Said Memorial Lecture at the AUB, focusing on the culture of empire and the responsibility of intellectuals. The lecture on May 10, entitled "Biolinguistic Explorations: Design, Development, Evolution," was a historical survey of central ideas of that field where linguistics, evolutionary biology, and the neurosciences all meet.

3. For a detailed and gripping account of the massacre and surrounding events, see Bayan Nuwayhed al-Hout, *Sabra and Shatila, September 1982* (London: Pluto Press, 2004). Two of the more trustworthy sources included in Bayan al-Hout's book are a report by the Lebanese Red Cross and an independent investigation by the Israeli journalist Amnon Kapeliouk. They note that between 3,000 and 3,500 people were murdered during the rampage on September 16–18, 1982. For a discussion of the wider political context, see Noam Chomsky, *Fateful Triangle, Updated Edition* (Boston, MA: South End Press, 1999); see, in particular, chapters 5 and 6.

4. Kinda's letter was reprinted in Noam Chomsky, *Pirates and Emperors* (New York: Claremont Research and Publications, 1986), 155. The letter and details of the whole episode are in a new edition of the book, Noam Chomsky, *Pirates and Emperors: Old and New, International Terrorism in the Real World* (Boston, MA: South End Press, 2002), 81–103. Charles Glass published Kinda's letter in the *Spectator*, London, May 3, 1986. A facsimile of the original was submitted to the mainstream press in the United States as a letter to the editor, but it wasn't published. The text was published by Alexander Cockburn in the monthly magazine *In These Times*, on July 23, 1986, with a suggestion that since President and Mrs. Reagan "are fond of reading out messages from small children, they might care to deliver this one on the next appropriate occasion."

5. The Shebaa Farms are a mountainside of little more than twenty-five square kilometers, occupied by Israel since 1967. From time to time, Lebanese shepherds and farmers who have lost their way into the Shebaa Farms have been abducted or killed by the Israeli army. It is one reason advanced by Hezbollah and its supporters for not giving up their weapons.

6. Bob Woodward and Charles R. Babcock, "CIA Tied to Beirut Bombing," *International Herald Tribune,* May 13, 1985.

7. Kilo is one of the signatories of a declaration entitled, "Beirut-Damascus/Damascus-Beirut," which appeared in the Beirut press on May 11, 2006. The declaration was signed by nearly 300 Lebanese and Syrian intellectuals, and called for a normalization of relations between Lebanon and Syria, based on respect for the independence and sovereignty of both countries. A few days after Kilo's arrest, several other of the Syrian signatories were also taken to prison.

2. Imminent Crises: Threats and Opportunities

1. See Aaron David Miller, *Search for Security* (Chapel Hill, NC: University of North Carolina Press, 1980); Irvine Anderson, *Aramco, the United States and Saudi Arabia* (Princeton, NJ: Princeton University Press, 1981); Michael Stoff, *Oil, War and American Security* (New Haven: Yale University Press, 1980); Steven Spiegel, *The Other Arab-Israeli Conflict* (Chicago: University of Chicago Press, 1985), 51.
2. *National Security Strategy of the United States* (Washington, DC: The White House, March 1990).
3. Alan Cowell, "Kurds Assert Few Outside Iraq Wanted Them to Win," *New York Times*, April 11, 1991.
4. Nina Kamp and Michael E. O'Hanlon, "The State of Iraq: An Update," *New York Times*, March 19, 2006.
5. Walter Pincus, "Skepticism about U.S. Deep, Iraq Poll Shows; Motive for Invasion Is Focus of Doubts," *Washington Post*, November 12, 2003; Richard Burkholder, "Gallup Poll of Baghdad: Gauging US Intent," *Government & Public Affairs*, October 28, 2003.
6. Michael MccGwire, "The Rise and Fall of the NPT: An Opportunity for Britain," *International Affairs* 81 (January 2005): 134.
7. Zbigniew Brzezinski, "Hegemonic Quicksand," *National Interest* 74 (Winter 2003/2004): 5–16; Stefan Wagstyl, "Cheney Rebukes Putin on Energy 'Blackmail,' " *Financial Times*, May 4, 2006.
8. See Ian Rutledge, *Addicted to Oil* (London: I. B. Tauris, 2005).
9. See *Multinational Oil Corporation and U.S. Foreign Policy*, *Report to the Committee on Foreign Relations*, U.S. Senate, January 2, 1975 (Washington DC: Government Printing Office, 1975).
10. Hal Weitzman, "Nationalism Fuels Fears over Morales' Power," *Financial Times*, May 2, 2006.
11. *National Security Strategy of the United States* (Washington DC: The White House, March 2006), 41.
12. David E. Sanger, "China's Rising Need for Oil Is High on U.S. Agenda," *New York Times*, April 18, 2006.
13. Editorial, *New York Times*, August 25, 1966.
14. Mark Curtis, *The Great Deception* (London: Pluto Press, 1998), 133.
15. Darna Linzer, "Past Arguments Don't Square with Current Iran Policy," *Washington Post*, March 27, 2005.
16. Mohamed ElBaradei, "Towards a Safer World," *The Economist*, October 16, 2003.
17. Frank von Hippel, "Coupling a Moratorium to Reductions as a First Step toward the Fissile-Material Cutoff Treaty," in Rakesh Sood, Frank von Hippel, and Morton Halperin, "The Road to Nuclear Zero: Three Approaches," Center for Advanced Study of India, 1998, 17; http://casi.ssc.upenn.edu/research/papers/Sood_1997.PDF.

18. See Rebecca Johnson, "2004 UN First Committee: Better Organised, with Deep Divisions," *Disarmament Diplomacy* 79 (April/May 2005), http://www.acronym.org.uk/dd/dd79/79unfc.htm; Jean du Preez, "The Fissban: Time for Renewed Commitment or a New Approach?," *Disarmament Diplomacy* 79 (April/May 2005), http://www.acronym.org.uk/dd/dd79/79jp.htm.
19. Martin van Creveld, "Sharon on the Warpath: Is Israel Planning to Attack Iran?" *International Herald Tribune*, August 21, 2004.
20. Jeffrey Fleishman and Alissa Rubin, "ElBaradei Asks for Restraint on Iran Sanctions," *Los Angeles Times*, March 31, 2006.
21. Michael MccGwire, "The Rise and Fall of the NPT: An Opportunity for Britain," *International Affairs* 81 (January 2005): 127; John Steinbruner and Nancy Gallagher, "Constructive Transformation: An Alternative Vision of Global Security," *Daedalus* 133, no. 3 (Summer 2004): 99; Sam Nunn, "The Cold War's Nuclear Legacy Has Lasted too Long," *Financial Times*, December 6, 2004.
22. National Intelligence Council, *Global Trends 2015: A Dialogue about the Future with Nongovernment Experts* (Washington DC, December 2000); U.S. Space Command, *Vision for 2020* (February 1997), 7; Pentagon, *Quadrennial Defense Review*, May 1997.
23. See Afaf Lutfi al-Sayyid Marsot, *Egypt in the Reign of Muhammad Ali* (New York: Cambridge University Press, 1984), 240; Harold Temperley, *England and the Near East: The Crimea* (London: Longmans, Green and Co., 1936).

3. The Great Soul of Power

1. Hans J. Morgenthau, "Reflections on the End of the Republic," *New York Review of Books* 15, no. 5 (September 24, 1970).
2. Michael Wines, "Two Views of Inhumanity Split the World, Even in Victory," *New York Times*, June 13, 1999.
3. James M. Goldgeier, Review of *Collision Course: NATO, Russia, and Kosovo* by John Norris, *Political Science Qaurterly* 121, no. 1 (Spring 2006): 179–181.
4. John Norris, *Collision Course: NATO, Russia, and Kosovo* (Westport, Conn.: Praeger, 2005), xxiii.
5. Elizabeth Becker, "Kissinger Tapes Describe Crises, War and Start Photos of Abuse," *New York Times*, May 27, 2004.
6. Noah Feldman, "Becoming bin Laden," *New York Times*, February 12, 2006.
7. Michael R. Gordon, "Allies Preparing for a Long Fight as Taliban Dig In," *New York Times*, October 28, 2001.
8. Kamil Mahdi, "The Iraqi Sanctions Debate: Destruction of a People," *Middle East International*, December 24, 1999.
9. Louis A. Pérez Jr., "Fear and Loathing of Fidel Castro: Sources of US Policy toward Cuba," *Journal of Latin American Studies* 34, no. 2 (May 2002): 227–254.
10. Quoted by Walter LaFeber, *America, Russia, and the Cold War* (New York: Wiley, 1967), 133.
11. Walter Lippmann, *The Essential Lippmann: A Political Philosophy for Liberal Democracy*, Clinton Rossiter and James Lare, eds. (Cambridge, MA: Harvard University Press, 1982), 91–2.
12. Michel Crozier, Samuel P. Huntington, and Joji Watanuki, *The Crisis of Democracy: Report on the Governability of Democracies to the Trilateral Commission* (New York: New York University Press, 1975).

13. David Ricardo, *The Works and Correspondence of David Ricardo*, vol. 1 (Cambridge: Cambridge University Press, 1951), 136–137.

14. Hans J. Morgenthau, *The Purpose of American Politics* (New York: Vintage, 1964).

15. John E. Rielly, ed., *American Public Opinion and U.S. Foreign Policy 1987* (Chicago: Chicago Council on Foreign Relations, 1987).

16. Morgenthau, *The Purpose of American Politics.*

17. Jonathan Monten, "The Roots of the Bush Doctrine: Power, Nationalism, and Democracy Promotion in U.S. Strategy," *International Security* 29, no. 4 (Spring 2005): 112.

18. Katerina Dalacoura, "US Democracy Promotion in the Arab Middle East Since 11 September 2001: A Critique," *International Affairs* 81, no. 5 (October 2005): 963–979.

19. David Ignatius, "A War of Choice, and One Who Chose It," *Washington Post*, November 2, 2003.

20. Thomas Carothers, *Critical Mission: Essays on Democracy Promotion* (Washington DC: Carnegie Endowment for International Peace, 2004), 7,42.

21. Thomas Carothers, "The Reagan Years: The 1980s," in Abraham F. Lowenthal, ed., *Exporting Democracy: The United States and Latin America* (Baltimore: Johns Hopkins University Press, 1991); Thomas Carothers, *In the Name of Democracy: U.S. Policy toward Latin America in the Reagan Years* (Berkeley: University of California Press, 1991).

22. Robert Pastor, *Condemned to Repetition: The United States and Nicaragua* (Princeton: Princeton University Press, 1987).

23. Lawrence R. Jacob and Benjamin I. Page, "Who Influences U.S. Foreign Policy?" *American Political Science Review* 99, no. 1 (February 2005): 107–123; see also Walter Lippmann, *Essays in the Public Philosophy* (Boston: Little, Brown, 1955).

24. William Stivers, *Supremacy and Oil: Iraq, Turkey, and the Anglo-American World Order, 1918–1930* (Ithaca, NY: Cornell University Press, 1982), 66–73.

25. Clive Ponting, *Churchill* (London: Sinclair-Stevenson 1994), 132; Winston Churchill, *The Second World War*, vol. 5 (Boston: Houghton Mifflin, 1951), 382.

26. Clive Ponting, *Churchill* (London: Sinclair-Stevenson, 1994), 132; Winston Churchill, *The World Crisis* (New York: Scribner, 1927).

27. Tsuyoshi Hasegawa, *Racing the Enemy* (Cambridge, MA: Harvard University Press, 2005).

28. Gordon Connell-Smith, *The Inter-American System* (London: Oxford University Press, 1966), 16; Stephen G. Rabe, *Eisenhower and Latin America: The Foreign Policy of Anticommunism* (Chapel Hill, NC: University of North Carolina Press, 1988), 33.

29. Frederick Kempe, "Thinking Global: U.S. Attempts to Coach China on New World Role; Americans Aim to Show Hu How His Country Can Act as 'Responsible Stakeholder,' " *Wall Street Journal*, April 18, 2006.

30. John Steinbruner and Nancy Gallagher, "Constructive Transformation: An Alternative Vision of Global Security," *Daedalus* 133, no. 3 (Summer 2004): 83–103.

31. John Stuart Mill, "A Few Words on Non-Intervention," *Fraser's Magazine* (December 1859).

32. Rudolf Rocker, *Anarcho-syndicalism* (London: Pluto Press, 1989).

33. Geoffrey Parker, *The Military Revolution: Military Innovation and the Rise of the West, 1500–1800* (Cambridge: Cambridge University Press, 1988).

34. V. G. Kiernan, *The Lords of Human Kind: Black Man, Yellow Man, and White Man in an Age of Empire* (Boston: Little, Brown, 1969).

5. Echoes from a Haunted Land

1. Bayan Nuwayed-al-Hout, *Sabra and Shatila, 1982* (London, UK: Pluto Press, 2004), 1.
2. Jeremy Harding, "Jeremy Harding Goes to Beirut to Meet Novelist Elias Khoury," *London Review of Books*, vol. 28., November 16, 2006.
3. Noam Chomsky, *The Fateful Triangle*, Updated Edition (Cambridge, MA: South End Press, 1999), 224.
4. Ibid., 197, 362.
5. Amnon Kapeliuk, *Enquête sur un massacre: Sabra et Chatilla* (Paris: Editions du Seuil, 1982), 93–94.
6. This and the citation that follows are taken from Colin Campbell, "Survivors of Massacre Tell of Reign of Terror," *The New York Times,* September 21, 1982, A18.
7. Chomsky, *The Fateful Triangle*, 364–5.
8. "Requiem, 1935-1940," cited in *Poems of Akhmatova*, trans. Stanley Kunitz with Max Hayward (Boston and New York: Houghton Mifflin Company, 1973), 99.
9. "Israel in Lebanon: Report of the International Commission to Enquire into Reported Violations of International Law by Israel during its Invasion of the Lebanon," established in 1982 by a group of internationally renowned jurists and public figures. Cited in *Journal of Palestine Studies*, vol. XII, no. 3, Spring 1983, 111; see also, The Complete Kahan Commission Report, *The Beirut Massacre* (Princeton and New York: Karz-Cohl Publishing, Inc., 1983); and Amnon Kapeliuk, *Enquête sur un Massacre* (Paris: Editions du Seuil, 1982), 1.
10. International Commission, *Journal of Palestine Studies*, 110.
11. Ze'ev Sternhell, "Resign! Reveal the Truth," *Ha'aretz*, Sept. 26, 1982, 9.
12. "Israel Outlines Terms for a Lebanon Security Zone," *The New York Times*, December 21, 1982, A9.
13. "18 Die as a Bomb Wrecks the P.L.O.'s Last Public Office in Beirut," *The New York Times*, February 6, 1982.
14. Wadie Said, "The Palestinians in Lebanon: The Rights of the Victims of the Palestinian-Israeli Peace Process," in *Columbia Human Rights Law Review*, vol. 30, no.2, Spring 1999.
15. Sara Roy, *Failing Peace, Gaza and the Palestinian-Israeli Conflict* (London: Pluto Press, 2007), 242.
16. Susan M. Akram and Terry Rempel, "Temporary Protection as an Instrument for Implementing the Right of Return for Palestinian Refugees," *Boston University International Law Journal,* vol. 22, no. 1, Spring 2004, 113, fn. 526. Population figures vary. I have relied on UNRWA's figures; these do not include Palestinian refugees who are not registered.
17. NSC 47/2, "A Report to the President by the National Security Council on United States Policy toward Israel and the Arab States," Oct. 17, 1949, Washington, D.C.
18. Akram and Rempel, *op. cit.,* 113. See footnote 527.
19. International Federation for Human Rights, *Lebanon: Palestinian Refugees* Report No. 356/2 (March 2003), 12.
20. Akram and Rempel, *op. cit.*, 115.
21. Ibid. See footnote 538.
22. William E. Farrell, "Palestinians in Lebanon Alarmed by Arrests and Rumors of Transfer," *The New York Times,* October 3, 1982, 20.

23. Interview with Sayyed Hassan Nasrallah and Noam Chomsky on May 11, 2006.

24. See Laleh Khalili, "The Refugees Who Give Refuge," in Reinaud Leenders, Amal Ghazal, and Jens Hanssen (eds.), *The Sixth War, Israel's Invasion of Lebanon*, MIT-EJMES (electronic journal of Middle East Studies), Summer 2006, 57–67.

25. Harding, *op. cit.*

26. Aviv Lavie, "Never, Never Land: On Khiam Prison in Southern Lebanon," *Middle East Report*, Spring 1997, 36.

27. Human Rights Watch, "Civilian Pawns, Laws of War Violations and the Use of Weapons on the Israel-Lebanon Border," May 1996, 16; available online at http://hrw.org/reports/1996/Israel.htm.

28. Lavie, *op. cit.*, 34.

29. Jim Quilty, "Prison. Museum. Ruin," *The Daily Star*, Beirut, August 24, 2006.

6. Meeting Sayyid Hassan Nasrallah: "Encounter with a Fighter"

1. Sayyid Hassan Nasrallah was elected secretary-general of Hezbollah a few years earlier, in 1992, after his predecessor Abbas Musawi was killed in a "target assassination" raid carried out by Israeli helicopter gunships (which also killed Musawi's wife and daughter and four others nearby).

2. Robert Fisk, "Hizbollah leader claims 'sad victory,' " *The Independent*, May 5, 1996; David Gardner, "Lebanon: A forceful national party," *The Financial Times*, July 16, 1996.

3. Eqbal Ahmad, "Encounter with a fighter," *Al-Ahram Weekly*, July 30–August 5, 1998; available online at http://weekly.ahram.org.eg/1998/388/re4.htm.

4. Seymour M. Hersh, "The Syrian Bet," *The New Yorker*, July 28, 2003.

5. Adam Shatz, "In Search of Hezbollah," *The New York Review of Books*, April 29, 2004.

6. Shatz's biases clearly come through in a later article, "Nasrallah's Game," *The Nation Online*, July 20, 2006 (http://www.thenation.com/doc/20060731/nasrallah_game). In this later article, Nasrallah is depicted as an adventurist, ready to engage in a high-risk gamble to preserve Hezbollah's weapons and prestige. Shatz's concluding statement is that Nasrallah is "someone who has no fear of death," and that Hezbollah's followers have a "passion for martyrdom." This is exactly the stuff peddled by most of the mainstream media, in perfect harmony with the party line from Washington.

7. Amy Goodman and Juan Gonzalez, "Hezbollah Leader Hassan Nasrallah Talks with Former U.S. Diplomats," *Democracy Now*, July 28, 2006; available online at http://democracynow.org/article.pl?sid=06/07/28/1440244. A former official of the U.S. government, Peck's pronouncements were startling in more than one way. For example, he made clear that the U.S. government, by its own definition of terrorism, is a terrorist organization:

   > In 1985, when I was the Deputy Director of the Reagan White House Task Force on Terrorism, they asked us—this is a Cabinet Task Force on Terrorism; I was the Deputy Director of the working group—they asked us to come up with a definition of terrorism that could be used throughout the government. We produced about six, and each and every case, they were rejected, because careful reading would indicate that our own country had been involved in some of those activities.

8. David Gardner, *op. cit.*

9. See Fawwaz Traboulsi, "The New Middle East," in this book.

10. Lin Noueihed, "Hizbollah sees no need to aid Iran if U.S. strikes," *Scotsman*, Reuters, May 22, 2006.
11. Amal Saad-Ghorayeb, "The Framing of Hezbollah," *The Guardian*, July 15, 2006.
12. Guy Dinmore, "Experts challenge White House line on Iran's influence," *The Financial Times*, July 18, 2006.
13. David Gardner, "A Modern Shiite: FT Interview Sheikh Hassan Nasrallah," *The Financial Times*, September 8, 1998.
14. David Ignatius, "Muslim Radicals in Power," *The Washington Post*, February 3, 2006.
15. Seymour Hersh, *op. cit.*
16. Adam Shatz, *op.cit.*
17. Amal Saad-Ghorayeb, "People say no: Public opinion in Lebanon overwhelmingly rejects U.S.-Israeli plans for cleansing Lebanon of Hezbollah," *Al-Ahram Weekly*, August 3–9, 2006.
18. We did not check the authenticity of the Israeli writings Nasrallah referred to. His associates, and others who have met him, say he is a voracious reader of Israeli politics and military affairs.
19. Robert Fisk, *op. cit.*
20. Eqbal Ahmad, *op. cit.*
21. Jonathan Finer and Molly Moore, "Israel Moves Thousands of Soldiers into Lebanon," *The Washington Post*, August 2, 2006.
22. Adam Shatz, *op. cit.*
23. Charles Glass, "Learning from Its Mistakes," *The London Review of Books*, Vol. 28, No. 16, August 17, 2006; available online at www.lrb.co.uk/v28/n16/glas01_.html.

7. On the U.S.-Israeli Invasion of Lebanon

1. Farah Stockman, "View of Common Fears Drives US-Israel Policy: Nations Seen Allied in Larger Struggle," *Boston Globe*, August 18, 2006.
2. "A Problem that Can't Be Ignored," *New York Times*, June 17, 2006.
3. See Aaron David Miller, *Search for Security* (Chapel Hill, NC: University of North Carolina Press, 1980); Irvine Anderson, *Aramco, the United States and Saudi Arabia* (Princeton, NJ: Princeton University Press, 1981); Michael Stoff, *Oil, War and American Security* (New Haven: Yale University Press, 1980); Steven Spiegel, *The Other Arab-Israeli Conflict* (Chicago: University of Chicago Press, 1985), 51.

Index

Page numbers in italics refer to photographs.